Senses of the Subject

JUDITH BUTLER

Senses of the Subject

Fordham University Press

New York   2015

Visit us online at www.fordhampress.com.

Library of Congress Cataloging-in-Publication Data available online at catalog.loc.gov.

Printed in the United States of America

17 16 15   5 4 3 2 1

First edition

CONTENTS

ACKNOWLEDGMENTS

I would like to thank the late and unforgettable Helen Tartar and Fordham University Press for making this collection possible, Zoe Weiman-Kelman and Aleksey Dubilet for helping with the manuscript preparation, and Bud Bynack for his tenacious and arresting editing. This tentative book is dedicated to Denise Riley, without whose thoughts I would not have very many of my own.

Although these texts evince overlapping and emergent themes, they differ substantially, given the nineteen years that passed between the earliest and the most recent writings included here (Kierkegaard in 1993 and Hegel in 2012). These essays were first printed in the following publications:

"How Can I Deny that These Hands and This Body Are Mine?," *Qui Parle* 11, no. 1 (1998); reprinted in expanded form in *Material Events: Paul de Man and the Afterlife of Theory* (Minneapolis: University of Minnesota Press, 2001); "Kierkegaard's Speculative Despair," in

Robert Solomon and Kathleen Higgins, eds., *German Idealism* (London: Routledge, 1993); "Merleau-Ponty and the Touch of Malebranche," in Taylor Carmen, ed., *Merleau-Ponty Reader* (London: Cambridge, 2005); "Sexual Difference as a Question of Ethics," in Laura Doyle, ed., *Bodies of Resistance* (Evanston: Northwestern University Press, 2001); "Spinoza's Ethics under Pressure," in Victoria Kahn, Neil Saccamano, and Daniela Coli, eds., *Politics and Passions* (Princeton: Princeton University Press, 2006); "Violence, Nonviolence: Sartre on Fanon," *Graduate Faculty Philosophy Journal* 27, no. 1 (2006); reprinted in Jonathan Judaken, ed., *Race after Sartre*, (Albany: State University of New York Press, 2008); *To Sense What Is Living in the Other: Hegel's Early Love*, dOCUMENTA (13) Notebooks, no. 66 (Hatje Cantz Verlag, 2012) (bilingual edition, English and German).

Judith Butler, Berkeley, 2014

Senses of the Subject

Introduction

This volume represents an array of philosophical essays that I have
written over the a period of twenty years (1993–2012), registering some
shifts in my views over that period of time.[1] If I am asked to say what,
if anything, rationalizes this collection, I could only answer in a faltering way. If there is a sense to be discerned from that faltering, it
would probably be this: when we speak about subject formation, we
invariably presume a threshold of susceptibility or impressionability
that may be said to precede the formation of a conscious and deliber-
ate "I." That means only that this creature that I am is affected by
something outside of itself, understood as prior, that activates and informs the subject that I am. When I make use of that first-person pronoun in this context, I am not exactly telling you about myself. Of
course, what I have to say has personal implications, but it operates at
a relatively impersonal level. So I do not always encumber the first-
person pronoun with scare quotes, but I am letting you know that when
I say "I," I mean you, too, and all those who come to use the pronoun

or to speak in a language that inflects the first person in a different way.

My point is to suggest that I am already affected before I can say "I" and that I have to be affected to say "I" at all. Those straightforward propositions fail, though, to describe the threshold of susceptibility that precedes any sense of individuation or linguistic capacity for self-reference. One could say that I am suggesting simply that the senses are primary and that we feel things, undergo impressions, prior to forming any thoughts, including any thoughts we might have about ourselves. That characterization would be true of what I have to say, but it would not fully enough explain what I hope to show.

First, I am not sure whether there are certain kinds of "thoughts" that operate in the course of sensing something. But second, I want to underscore the methodological problem that emerges for any such claim about the primacy of the senses: if I say that I am already affected before I can say "I," I am speaking much later than the process I seek to describe. In fact, my retrospective position casts doubt on whether or not I can describe this situation at all, since strictly speaking, I was not present for the process, and I myself seem to be one of its various effects. Further, it may be that retroactively, I reconstitute that origin according to whatever phantasm grips me, and so you will receive an account only of my phantasm, not of my origin. Given how vexed they are, one might think we should all remain silent on such matters, avoiding the first person altogether, since the indexical function fails precisely at the moment in which we want to marshal its forces to help us describe something difficult. My suggestion, rather, is that we accept this belatedness and proceed in a narrative fashion that marks the paradoxical condition of trying to relate something about my formation that is prior to my own narrative capacity and that, in fact, brings that narrative capacity about.

Let us follow Nietzsche's well-known remark that the bell that has "boomed . . . the twelve beats of noon" startles the self-reflective person who only *afterward* rubs his ears and, "surprised and disconcerted," asks, "what really was that which we have just experienced?"[2] It may be that this kind of belatedness, what Freud called "Nachträglichkeit," is an inevitable feature of inquiries such as these, inflecting the narration with the historical perspective of the present. Still, is it possible to try to give a narrative sequence for the process of being affected, a threshold of susceptibility and transfer and I that might reflect upon and relay, a life that did not yet exist and that, in part, accounts for the emergence of that I?

Certain literary fictions rely on these kinds of impossible scenarios. Consider the rather fantastic beginning of David Copperfield, in which the narrator speaks with extraordinary perspicacity about the details of ordinary life preceding and including his own birth. He mentions parenthetically that he has been told the story of his birth and that he believes what he has been told, but as the narration proceeds, he ceases to relay the story as if it were authored by someone other than himself; he has inserted himself as a knowing narrator at the very outset of his life, a way perhaps to get around the difficulty of once having been an infant unable to speak, reflect, or think as an adult author does. A certain denial of infancy seeps into his ever more authoritative account of when he cried and what others thought and did on that occasion.

Indeed, the opening chapter is fantastically entitled "I Am Born," and the very first line throws down the gauntlet: Will this narrator be authored, or will he author himself? The novel opens: "Whether I shall turn out to be the hero of my own life, or whether that station will be held by anybody else, these pages must show." There is, of course, a double irony, given that the narrator is a fictional construct of Charles Dickens and so already and continuously authored, even as he poses this question, suggesting that he might be able to leap out of the text that supports his fictional existence. Even within the terms of the novel, it is obvious that he could not have offered a report on his own birth with any kind of first-hand authority, and yet he proceeds with this impossible and seductive undertaking precisely as if he were there, looking on, as it were, as he enters the world.

Narrative authority does not require being at the scene. It requires only that one is able to reconstruct the scene from a position of non-presence in a believable way or that one's unbelievable narration is compelling for its own reasons. The story means something as he relates it, since we are being introduced into his rather remarkable self-understanding. What he relates may or may not be true, but it hardly matters, once we understand that the story he reaches for says something about his authorial ambitions and desires, clearly meant to counter and displace the infant's passivity and the lack of motor control, a resistance perhaps to needing to be in the hands of those he never chose, who turned out to care for him more or less well.

My point is not to say that what happens in literary works such as these has a parallel in the theory of subject formation. Rather, I want to suggest that narrative gestures such as these find their place in nearly any theory of subject formation. Could it be that the narrative dimension of the theory of subject formation is impossible, yet necessary, inevitably belated, especially when the task is to discern how the subject is initially animated by what affects it and how these transitive processes are reiterated in the animated life that follows? If we want to talk about these matters, we have to agree to occupy an impossible position, one that, perhaps, repeats the impossibility of the condition we seek to describe.

To say that it is impossible does not mean that it cannot be done, but only that we cannot quite find a way out of the constraints of adult life except by asking how those incipient passages remain with us, recurring still and again. To say that I am affected prior to ever becoming an "I" is to deliver the news by using the very pronoun that was not yet put into play, confounding this temporality with that one. I, personally, cannot go back to that place, nor can I do so in an impersonal way. And yet there seems to be much we can still say. For instance, let us think about the language in which we come to describe the emergence or formation of the subject.

In a theoretical vein, we can, following a general Foucaultian line, simply state that the subject is produced through norms or by discourse more generally. If we slow down and ask what is meant by "produced" and to what view of production does such a passive verb formation belong, we find that there is much work to be done. Is "being produced" the same as "being formed," and does it matter which locution we use? It is always possible to refer to a norm as a singular kind of thing, but let us remember that norms tend to arrive in clusters, interconnected, and that they have both spatial and temporal dimensions inseparable from what they are, how they act, and how they form what they act upon.

A norm may be said to precede us, to circulate in the world before it touches upon us. When it does make its landing, it acts in several different ways: norms impress themselves upon us, and that impression opens up an affective register. Norms form us, but only because there is already some proximate and involuntary relation to their impress; they require and intensify our impressionability. Norms act on us from all sides, that is, in multiple and sometimes contradictory ways; they act upon a sensibility at the same time that they form it; they lead us to feel in certain ways, and those feelings can enter into our thinking even, as we might well end up thinking about them. They condition and form us, and yet they are hardly finished with that work once we start to emerge as thinking and speaking beings. Rather, they continue to act according to an iterative logic that ends for any of us only when life ends, though the life of norms, of discourse more generally, continues on with a tenacity that is quite indifferent to our finitude. Foucault clearly knew this when he remarked that discourse is not life: its time is not ours.[3]

We tend to make a mistake when, in trying to explain subject formation, we imagine a single norm acting as a kind of "cause" and then imagine the "subject" as something formed in the wake of that norm's action. Perhaps what we are trying to describe is not exactly a causal series. I do not arrive in the world separate from a set of norms that are lying in wait for me, already orchestrating my gender, race, and status, working on me, even as a pure potential, prior to my first wail. So norms, conventions, institutional forms of power, are already acting prior to any action I may undertake, prior to there being an "I" who thinks of itself from time to time as the seat or source of its own action. My point is not to make a mockery of such moments in which we understand ourselves to be the source of our own actions. We have to do that if we are to understand ourselves as agentic at all. The task is to think of being acted on and acting as simultaneous, and not only as a sequence. Perhaps it is a repeated predicament: to be given over to a world in which one is formed even as one acts or seeks to bring something new into being. Acting does not liberate any of us from our formations, despite the protestations of gleeful existentialism. Our formation does not suddenly fall away after certain breaks or ruptures; they become important to the story we tell about ourselves or to other modes of self-understanding. There remains that history from which I broke, and that breakage installs me here and now. And so I am not really thinkable without that formation. At the same time, nothing determines me in advance—I am not formed once and definitively, but continuously or repeatedly. I am still being formed as I form myself in the here and now. And my own self-formative activity—what some would call "self-fashioning"—becomes part of that ongoing formative process. I am never simply formed, nor am I ever fully self-forming. This may be another way of saying that we live in historical time or that it lives in us as the historicity of whatever form we take as human creatures.

Finally, my argument would not be complete if I did not say that the contours of an ethical relationship emerge from this ongoing paradox of subject formation. I am affected not just by this one other or a set of others, but by a world in which humans, institutions, and organic and inorganic processes all impress themselves upon this me who is, at the outset, susceptible in ways that are radically involuntary. The condition of the possibility of my exploitation presupposes that I am a being in need of support, dependent, given over to an infrastructural world in order to act, requiring an emotional infrastructure to survive. I am not only already in the hands of *someone* else before I start to work with my own hands, but I am also, as it were, in the "hands" of institutions, discourses, environments, including technologies and life processes, handled by an organic and inorganic object field that exceeds the human. In this sense, "I" am nowhere and nothing without the nonhuman.

The unwilled character of this dependency is not itself exploitation, but it is a domain of dependency that is open to exploitation, as we know. Further, susceptibility is not the same as subjugation, though it can clearly lead there precisely when susceptibility is exploited (as often happens when we consider the exploitation of children, which depends on an exploitation of their dependency and the relatively uncritical dimensions of their trust). Susceptibility alone does not explain passionate attachment or falling in love, a sense of betrayal or abandonment. Yet all those ways of feeling can follow, depending on what happens in relation to those who move and affect us and who are susceptible to us (even susceptible to our susceptibility, a circle that accounts for certain forms of affective and sexual intensity). In each of these cases, it is less a causal series than a form of transitivity at work in delineating a set of relations; we do not always know, or cannot always say, who touched whom first, or what was the moment of being touched and what was the moment of touching. This is the consequential insight of Merleau-Ponty's "The Intertwining" from *The Visible and the Invisible*. It is also related to his more general account of how it is we come to sense anything at all, when he considers, in Malebranche, that being touched first animates the sentient subject.

Is something relayed or transferred in transitive relations such as these? Jean Laplanche would claim that there are enigmatic messages that are relayed at the early stages of infancy and that they become

installed as primary signifiers that launch the life of desire. The drives
are awakened by these strange early interpellations, and that enigmatic
quality persists throughout the trajectory of sexual desire: "What is
it that I want?"; "What is this in me that wants in the way it does?"[4]
For Merleau-Ponty and, indeed, with Malebranche, it is only by being acted on that any of us come to act at all. And when we do act,
we do not precisely overcome the condition of being acted upon. Being touched or handled or addressed as an infant awakens the senses,
paving the way for a sentient apprehension of the world.[5] And so, prior
to sensing anything at all, I am already in relation not only to one
particular other, but to many, to a field of alterity that is not restrictively human. Those relations form a matrix for subject formation,
which means that someone must first sense me before I can sense anything at all. Acted upon, quite without any consent, and surely through
no will of my own, I become the kind of being with the capacity to
sense something and to act. Even as I come to speak within a discourse
that firmly lodges the "I" at the source of its distinct action, I see that
this "I" remains in thrall to a prior transitivity, acted upon as it acts.
I cannot see this at all unless my ability to sense things has already
been animated by a set of others and conditions that are emphatically
not me. This is just another way of saying that no one transcends the
matrix of relations that gives rise to the subject; no one acts without
first being formed as one with the capacity to act.

Of course, many people do act *as if* they were not formed, and that
is an interesting posture to behold. To posit that capacity to act as a
fully independent feature of one's individuality (with no account of
individuation) is to engage in a form of disavowal that seeks to wish
away primary and enduring modes of dependency and interdependency,
including those disturbed conditions of abandonment or loss regis-
tered at early ages that are not precisely overcome or transcended in
the life that follows, but repeat through more or less unconscious en-
actments of various kinds. Certain versions of the sovereign "I" are
supported by that denial, which means, of course, that they are thor-

oughly brittle, often displaying that brittle insistence in symptomatic ways. Story lines ensue: When will that figure break of its own accord, or what will it have to destroy to support its image of self-sovereignty?

So perhaps it might be said that throughout these essays, a struggle with that form of sovereign individualism is underway. To claim that a subject acts only when it is first formed as a subject with the capacity to act, that is, as one who is already and still acted upon, might seem like a relatively conservative claim. Is it not possible to overcome our formation, to break with that matrix that formed any of us as a subject?

Of course, it is possible to break with certain norms as they exercise the power to craft us, but that can happen only by the intervention of countervailing norms. And if the latter can and does happen, it means simply that the "matrix of relations" that forms the subject is not an integrated and harmonious network, but a field of potential disharmony, antagonism, and contest. It also means that at moments of significant shift or rupture, we may not know precisely who we are or what is meant by "I" when we say it. If the "I" is separated from the "you" or indeed the "they," that is, from those without whom the "I" has been unthinkable, then there is doubtless a rather severe disorientation that follows. Who is this "I" in the aftermath of such a break with those constituting relations, and what, if anything, can it still become?

And it might be that the constituting relations have a certain pattern of breakage in them, that they actually constitute and break us at the same time. This makes for a tentative or more definitive form of madness, to be sure. What does it mean to require what breaks you? If the dependency on those others was once a matter of survival and now continues to function psychically as a condition of survival (recalling and reinstituting that primary condition), then certain kinds of breaks will raise the question of whether the "I" can survive.

Matters become more complex if one makes the break precisely in order to survive (breaking with what breaks you). In such situations, the "I" may undergo radically conflicting responses: as a consequence of its rupture with those formative relations, it will not survive; only with such a rupture does it now stand a chance to survive. The ambiguity attests to the fact that the "I" is not easily separated from those relations that made the "I" possible, but also to the reiteration of those relations and the possibility of a break that becomes part of its history, one that actually opens up a livable future. Frantz Fanon interrogates this problem of breaking with the terms of interpellation that institute one's "nonbeing" in order to break into the category of the human, even break it open by rejecting its racialized criteria. Similarly, Fanon underscores the conditions under which racialization establishes a kind of being who is destroyed prior to the very possibility of living and who must, in order to live, draw upon and develop another understanding of embodied freedom. For Fanon, as for Spinoza, the question also emerges: What destroys a person when that person appears to be destroying himself or herself? Do we find the social within the psychic at such moments, and if so, how? Strictly speaking, Spinoza believes that a person cannot take his or her own life, but that something external is working on the person at such moments. This raises the question of how what is "external" becomes not only "internal," but the driving force of psychic life.

To make this argument well, I would need to include a chapter on psychoanalysis, but that will not be found in this particular volume. The essay on Spinoza, however, does allow for a conjectured exchange between Spinoza and Freud. And yet many issues raised by psychoanalysis are interrogated in the texts considered here, including the condition of embodiment, the strategies of denial, primary dependency, the aims of desire, violence, and the primary importance of relationality and the persistently vexed character of social bonds and the unconscious.

The essays included here not only span nearly twenty years, but they represent less known—and less popular—dimensions of my philosophical work. The links to feminism and gender studies can be found in the essay on Merleau-Ponty and Irigaray, and some of my political commitments can surely be discerned in the essay on Sartre and Fanon, and also on Spinoza and the formulation of an ethics under pressure. But in the work on Malebranche in relation to Merleau-Ponty, Kierkegaard, Descartes, and Hegel, I am perhaps concerned more with the relational dimensions of embodiment: passion, desire, touch. I am less concerned with understanding the activities of the thinking "I" than with the sensuous conditions of being sensed and sensing, a transitive and ongoing paradoxical condition that continues even in the most self-sufficient postures of thought.

Again, the point is not to undermine any conceit we may have that we act or desire independently and to show that we are but the effects or prior and more powerful forces. Rather, the task is to see that what we call "independence" is always established through a set of formative relations that do not simply fall away as action takes place, even though those formative relations sometimes are banished from consciousness, even arguably *must be* banished to some extent. If I can come to touch and feel and sense the world, it is only because this "I," before it could be called an "I," was handled and sensed, addressed, and enlivened. The "I" never quite overcomes that primary impressionability, even though it might be said to be its occasional undoing. Oddly, but importantly, if the thesis is right, then the "I" comes into sentient being, even thinking and acting, precisely by being acted on in ways that, from the start, presume that nonvoluntary, though volatile field of impressionability. Already undone, or undone from the start, we are formed, and as formed, we come to be always partially undone by what we come to sense and know.

What follows is that form of relationality that we might call "ethical": a certain demand or obligation impinges upon me, and the response relies on my capacity to affirm this having been acted on, formed into one who can respond to this or that call. Aesthetic relationality also follows: something impresses itself upon me, and I develop impressions that cannot be fully separated from what acts on me. I am only moved or unmoved by something outside that impinges upon me in a more or less involuntary way.

This uneasy and promising relation cannot be easily denied, and if denial does prove possible, it comes at the cost of destroying a social and relational world. I would say that we must affirm the way we are already and still acted on in order to affirm ourselves, but self-affirmation means affirming the world without which the self would not be, and that means affirming what I could never choose, that is, what happens to me without my willing that precipitates my sensing and knowing the world as I do.

The ethical does not primarily describe conduct or disposition, but characterizes a way of understanding the relational framework within which sense, action, and speech become possible. The ethical describes a structure of address in which we are called upon to act or to respond in a specific way. Even at the preverbal level, the structure of address is still operative, which means that ethical relationality calls upon this domain or prior susceptibility.[6] One is called a name or addressed as "you" prior to any sense of individuation, and that calling, especially as it is repeated and rehearsed in different ways, starts to form a subject who calls itself by those same terms, learning how to shift the "you" to an "I" or to a gendered third person, a "he" or a "she." There is always disturbance in that shift, which is why self-reference, enabled by the scene of address, can and does take on meanings that exceed the aims of those who introduced the terms of discourse through address. So addressing someone as "you" may well solicit a recognition that it is "I" who is meant by that second person, but that "I" may well resist or shift or reject the various semantics that get associated with that "you." In other words, "Yes, it is me, but I am not the one you think I am."

This misrecognition at the heart of the scene of address becomes more stark when it is a matter of gender. If I do not recognize myself as "she," does that mean that I fail to recognize that someone seeks to interpellate me within that pronoun? I could act as if I am not being addressed, or I can turn around and offer the clarification of the pronoun I prefer, but whatever I do, I understand that that particular misrecognition was intended for me. In other words, even when the interpellation is wrong, it still is directed toward me. And sometimes when the interpellation is meant for someone else, and I think it is meant for me, it may be that the specific scene of address is misunderstood only because a more general scene of address is understood. Perhaps the catcall on the street was meant for one woman, and another understood that it was meant for her. The fact is that it probably could have been meant for the second woman, even as she was mistaken in this particular instance. Such interpellations are roving and overinclusive; they take any number of objects, even as they seem to be directed toward one. The relatively impersonal character of the interpellation means that misrecognition is always possible.[7] Further, it is not just the catcall or the insult or the slur that constitutes an interpellation within the scene of address; every pronoun has an interpellative force and carries with it the possibility of misrecognition: "You, you are the person I said I love?" or "I, I am the person you claim to love?"[8]

How does this discussion of interpellation relate to the issues of primary impressionability and subject formation? In the first instance, the scene of address and even its linguistic structure precede any act of vocalization. Address can take place through other kinds of signifying actions, through touch, movement, holding, by turning one way or another, achieving and losing visual or tactile connection. The question of whether someone else is present can raise the question of whether I am present, as if absence or presence were transitive spaces, intermediary zones between differentiated individuals. A vast potential for vacillation emerges in response to the question of whether there is an "I" that can be at once differentiated and dependent or is in the process of differentiating within dependency. The "I" may feel that it is nothing without the "you," and that may well index a very real condition of primary dependency (an early autobiographical condition relived psychically). Differentiation seems to thrive on the constitutive possibility of misrecognition that exists within any interpellation. Although a preverbal infant does not say, "Is it me you are calling when you say that name?" there is nevertheless something enigmatic at work in being called any name or assigned a gender through pronominal reference or repeated treatment and practice.[9] Both the proper name and gender must surely arrive as enigmatic noise that requires an interpretive response, which includes a series of errors and misrecognitions. Perhaps some sense of that enigma survives into the world of adult interpellations: "Is that me to whom you refer when you claim that I am this or that?" Sometimes the possibility of misrecognition emerges in the midst of the most intimate relations: "I cannot believe you are my mother!" or "Is this my child?"[10]

Although the "subject" usually refers to a linguistic creature already differentiated within language, even capable of linguistic self-reference, it presupposes subject formation, including an account of coming into language. The fact that language precedes the subject does not obviate the need to account for how language emerges and how to account for the relation between embodiment and language in subject formation. After all, if the scene of address is not necessarily verbal, and if it is not restrictively linguistic, then it designates a more primary operation of the discursive field at the level of the body. That said, we cannot really differentiate between different "levels" as if they had an ontological status that exceeds their heuristic utility. The body is always supported (or not supported) by technologies, structures, institutions, an array of others both personally and impersonally related, organic and life processes, to mention just a few of the conditions of emergence. Those supports are not simply passive structures. A support must *support*, and so must both be and act. A support cannot support without supporting *something*, so it is defined as both relational and agentic. So the transitive relay of agency has to be understood as happening somewhere in this zone where supports are already acting on a body with various degrees of success and failure, acting on a localized field of impressionability for which the distinction between passivity and activity is not quite stable and cannot be. Acted on, animated, and acting; addressed, animated, and addressing; touched, animated, and now sensing. These triads are partially sequential and partially chiasmic. And the same can be said about the relation between the body and language. After all, the throat and the hands signify want or frustration or pleasure prior to when any linguistic form of speech gives expressions to those dispositions. It is hardly controversial to claim that in infancy, a great deal of bodily signifying happens prior to vocalization and speech. The emergence of speech does not constitute a substitution and displacement of the body. Bodily significations do not become successfully converted or sublimated into speech; the bodily dimension of signification does not fall away as talking begins (nor does it haunt speech as a metaphysics of presence). Although bodies can be signifying one way and speech another, the two modalities remain related to one another, even if in symptomatic ways. (Hysteria is a prime instance.) At a more mundane level, a public speaker must find a way to animate the throat, or the person using sign language must figure out the right ways to move those hands. So though we might say that bodily signifying precedes speech, we would be mistaken to think that it vanishes with the speech act or, indeed, with the written text. In its absence, the body still signifies. Descartes tried not to know this, but, according to Nancy, his own language worked against that disavowal.[11]

Just as philosophy founders time and again on the question of the body, it tends to separate what is called thinking from what is called sensing, from desire, passion, sexuality, and relations of dependency. It is one of the great contributions of feminist philosophy to call those dichotomies into question and so to ask as well whether in sensing, something called thinking is already at work, whether in acting, we are also acted upon, and whether in coming into the zone of the thinking and speaking I, we are at once radically formed and also bringing something about. The primary impressions we receive establish a relationship of animated necessity with the world. We speak as if impressions are received or impressions are formed, but if they are formed as they are received, then primary impressionability gives us a way to rethink both activity and passivity, that dualism so problematically associated with gender difference. Even if we cannot return to primary impressionability as an originary condition except through fantastic narrative turns, that is no reason to dispute its importance. It just affirms that we require forms of fiction to arrive at self-understanding and that verification cannot operate in the usual way in this domain. If one seeks to give an account of a condition in which series and sequence were themselves a rather stark problem, as was the distinction between active and passive, then one has to find other means or allow for narrative to bespeak its own impossibility. Either way, it seems that we can understand neither what sense the subject might have nor how the subject comes to sense its world if we do not seek to describe the chiasmic conditions of its formation. This is not a matter of discovering and exposing an origin or tracking a causal series, but of describing what acts when I act, without precisely taking responsibility for the whole show. Where the ethical does enter, it seems, is precisely in that encounter that confronts me with a world I never chose, occasioning that affirmation of involuntary exposure to otherness as the condition of relationality, human and nonhuman. Acted on, I act still, but it is hardly this "I" that acts alone, and even though, or precisely because, it never quite gets done with being undone.

"How Can I Deny That These Hands and This Body Are Mine?"

I remember a sleepless night last year when I came into my living room and turned on the television set to discover that C-Span was offering a special session on feminist topics and that the historian Elizabeth Fox-Genovese was making clear why she thought Women's Studies had continuing relevance and why she opposed certain radical strains in feminist thinking. Of those positions she most disliked, she included the feminist view that no stable distinction between the sexes could be drawn or known, a view that suggests that the difference between the sexes is itself culturally variable, or, worse, discursively fabricated, as if it is all a matter of language. Of course, this did not help my project of falling asleep, and I became aware of being, as it were, a sleepless body in the world accused, at least obliquely, with having made the body less, rather than more relevant. Indeed, I was not altogether sure that the bad dream from which I had awoken some hours earlier was not in some sense being further played out on the screen. Was I waking, or was I dreaming? After all, it was no doubt the persecutory dimension of paranoia that hounded me from the bed. Was it still paranoia to think that she was talking about me, and was there really any way to know? If it was me, then how would I know that I am the one to whom she refers?

I relate this incident not only because it foreshadows the Cartesian dilemmas with which I will be preoccupied in the following paper and not because I propose to answer the question of whether sexual difference is only produced in language. I will, for the moment, leave the question of sexual difference, to be returned to another time.[1] The problem I do propose to address emerges every time we try to describe the *kind of action* that language exercises on the body or, indeed, in the production or maintenance of bodies. And we do tend to describe language as actively producing or crafting a body every time we use, implicitly or explicitly, the language of discursive construction.

In the consideration of Descartes's *Meditations* that follows, I propose to ask whether the way in which Descartes posits the irreality of his own body does not allegorize a more general problem of positing that is to be found in various forms of constructivism and various critical rejoinders to a constructivism that is sometimes less well understood than it ought to be. The name of this paper that I have already begun, but not yet begun, is: "How can I deny that these hands and this body are mine?" These are, of course, Descartes's words, but they could be ours or, indeed, mine, given the dilemmas posed by contemporary constructivism.

The language of discursive construction takes various forms in contemporary scholarship, and sometimes it does seem as if the body is created ex nihilo from the resources of discourse. To claim, for instance, that the body is fabricated in discourse is not only to figure discourse as a fabricating kind of activity, but to sidestep the important questions of "in what way" and "to what extent." To say that the line between the sexes, for instance, must be drawn, and must be drawable, is to concede that at some level the stability of the distinction depends upon a line being drawn. But to say that we must be able to draw a line in order to stabilize the distinction between the sexes may simply mean that we must first grasp this distinction in a way that allows us then to draw the line, and the drawing of the line confirms a distinction that is somehow already at hand. But it may mean, conversely, that there are certain conventions that govern how and where the line ought or ought not to be drawn and that these conventions, as conventions, change through time and produce a sense of anxiety and of unknowingness precisely at the moment in which we are compelled to draw a line in reference to the sexes. The line then lets us know what will and will not qualify as "sex"; the line works as a regulatory ideal, in Foucault's sense, or a normative criterion that permits and controls the appearance and knowability of sex. Then the question, which is not easily settled, becomes: Do the conventions that demarcate sexual difference determine in part what we "see" and "comprehend" as sexual difference? It is, you might surmise, not a large leap from this claim to the notion that sexual difference is fabricated in language. But I think that we may need to move more carefully before either championing or reviling this conclusion.

The language of construction risks a certain form of linguisticism, the assumption that what is constructed by language is therefore also language, that the object of linguistic construction is nothing other than language itself. Moreover, the action of this construction is conveyed through verbal expressions that sometimes imply a simple and unilateral creation at work. Language is said to fabricate or to figure the body, to produce or construct it, to constitute or to make it. Thus, language is said to act, which involves a tropological understanding of language as performing and performative. There is, of course, something quite scandalous involved in the strong version of construction that is sometimes at work when, for instance, the doctrine of construction implies that the body is not only made *by* language, but made *of* language or that the body is somehow reducible to the linguistic coordinates by which it is identified and identifiable, as if there is no nonlinguistic stuff at issue. The result is not only an ontological realm

understood as so many effects of linguistic monism, but the tropological functioning of language as action becomes strangely literalized
in the description of what it does and how it does what it does. And
though Paul de Man often argued that the tropological dimension of
discourse works against the performative, it seems here that we see, as
I believe we do in de Man's discussion of Nietzsche, the literalization
of the trope of performativity.

I want to suggest another way of approaching this question, which
refuses the reduction of linguistic construction to linguistic monism
and which calls into question the figure of language acting unilaterally and unequivocally on the object of construction. It may be that
the very term "construction" no longer makes sense in this context,
that the term "deconstruction" is better suited to what I propose to
describe, but I confess to not really caring about how or whether these
terms are stabilized in relation to one another, or, indeed, in relation
to me. My concerns are of another order, perhaps in the very tension
that emerges as the problem of discursive construction comes into dialogue with deconstruction.

For my purposes, I think it must be possible to claim that the body
is not known or identifiable apart from the linguistic coordinates that
establish the boundaries of the body—*without* thereby claiming that
the body is nothing other than the language by which it is known.
This last claim seeks to make the body an ontological effect of the
language that governs its knowability. Yet this view fails to note the
incommensurability between the two domains, an incommensurability that is not precisely an opposition. Although one might accept the
proposition that the body is knowable only through language, that *the
body is given through language*, it is never fully given in that way, and to say
that it is given partially can be understood only if we also acknowledge that it is given, when it is given, in parts—it is, as it were, given
and withheld at the same time, and language might be said to perform both of these operations. Although the body depends on language to be known, the body also exceeds every possible linguistic effort

of capture. It would be tempting to conclude that this means that the body exists outside of language, that it has an ontology separable from any linguistic one, and that we might be able to describe this separable ontology.

But this is where I would hesitate, perhaps permanently, for as we begin that description of what is outside of language, the chiasm reappears: we have already contaminated, though not contained, the very body we seek to establish in its ontological purity. The body escapes its linguistic grasp, but so, too, does it escape the subsequent effort to determine ontologically that very escape. The very description of the extralinguistic body allegorizes the problem of the chiasmic relation between language and body and so fails to supply the distinction it seeks to articulate.

To say that the body is figured chiasmically is to say that the following logical relations hold simultaneously: the body is given through language, but is not, for that reason, reducible to language. The language through which the body emerges helps to form and establish that body in its knowability, but the language that forms the body does not fully or exclusively form it. Indeed, the movement of language that appears to create what it names, its operation as a seamless performative of the illocutionary persuasion, covers over or dissimulates the substitution, the trope, by which language appears as a transitive act, that is, by which language is mobilized as a performative that simultaneously does what it says. If language acts on the body in some way—if we want to speak, for instance, of a bodily inscription, as so much cultural theory does—it might be worth considering whether language literally acts on a body and whether that body is an exterior surface for such action, or whether these are figures that we mobilize when we seek to establish the efficacy of language.

This leads to a converse problem, namely, the case in which language attempts to deny its own implication in the body, in which the case for the radical disembodiment of the soul is made within language. Here, it is a question of the way in which the body emerges in the very language that seeks to deny it, which suggests that no operation of language can fully separate itself from the operation of the body. Language itself cannot proceed without positing the body, and when it tries to proceed as if the body were not essential to its own operation, figures of the body reappear in spectral and partial form within the very language that seeks to perform their denial. Thus, language cannot escape the way in which it is implicated in bodily life, and when it attempts such an escape, the body returns in the form of spectral figures whose semantic implications undermine the explicit claims of disembodiment made within language itself. Thus, just as the effort to determine the body linguistically fails to grasp what it names, so the effort to establish that failure as definitive is undermined by the figural persistence of the body.

This chiasmic relation becomes clear through a reconsideration of the opening *Meditations* of Descartes, wherein he calls the reality of his body into question. Descartes seeks to know whether he can deny the reality of his own body and, in particular, the reality of his limbs.[2] For the moment, though, I want to suggest that Descartes's ability to doubt the body appears to prefigure the skeptical stance toward bodily reality that is often associated with contemporary constructionist positions. What happens in the course of Descartes's fabulous trajectory of doubt is that the very language through which he calls the body into question ends by reasserting the body as a condition of his own writing. Thus, the body that comes into question as an "object" that may be doubted surfaces in the text as a figural precondition of his writing.

But what is the status of Cartesian doubt, understood as something that takes place in writing, in a writing that we read and that, in reading, we are compelled to reperform? Derrida raises the question of whether the Cartesian "I" is compatible with the method of doubt, if that method is understood as transposable, one that anyone might perform. A method must be repeatable or iterable; intuition (or self-inspection) requires the singularity of the mind under inspection. How can a method be made compatible with the requirements of introspection? Although Descartes's meditative method is an introspective one in which he seeks in an unmediated fashion to know himself, it is also one that is written and that is apparently performed in the very temporality of writing. Significantly, he does not report in language the various introspective acts that he has performed prior to the writing: the writing appears as contemporaneous with this introspection, implying, contrary to his explicit claims, that meditation is not an unmediated relation at all, but one that must and does take place through language.

As is well known, Descartes begins his *Meditations* by seeking to eradicate doubt. Indeed, he begins in an autobiographical mode, asking how long it has been that he sensed that many of his beliefs were false, these beliefs that he held in the past, that appeared to be part of his youth, that were part of his history. He then seeks to "rid himself" of his former beliefs or "undo" them (*"défaire de toutes les opinions que j'avais reçues"*).[3] First, he claims: "I have delivered my mind from every care," and he is, apparently luckily, "agitated by no passions," free to "address myself to the upheaval (*destruction*) of all my former opinions."[4] (His task is the dispassionate destruction of his own opinion, but also of his own past, and so we might understand the onset of the *Meditations* to require performing a destruction of one's own past, of memory). Thus, an "I" emerges, narratively, at a distance from its former opinions, shearing off its historicity and inspecting and adjudicating its beliefs from a care-free position. Whatever the "I" is, it is from the start not the same as the beliefs that it holds and that it scrutinizes; or rather, the "I" appears to be able to maintain itself, at the level of grammar, while it calls such beliefs into question. To call such beliefs into question is apparently not to call the "I" into question. The one, the "I," is manifestly distinct from the beliefs that this "I" has held.

We must then, as readers, in order to follow this text, imagine an "I" who is detachable from the history of its beliefs. And the grammar asks us to do this prior to the official beginning of the method of doubt. Moreover, the very term that is generally translated as "belief" is *opinions* and so implies a kind of groundless knowing from the start, a form of knowing whose groundlessness will be exposed.

Descartes seeks the principles of his former beliefs, finds that relying on the senses produces deception, and argues that nothing that once produced deception ought to be trusted again to furnish anything other than deception in the future. And yet, sometimes the senses furnish a certain indubitability, as when the narrator relays the following famous scene: there is the fact that leads Descartes to say, "I am here, seated by the fire, attired in a dressing gown, having this paper in my hands and other similar matters."[5] Let me call attention to the fact that the "I" is "here," *ici,* because this term in this sentence is a deictic one; it is a shifter, pointing to a "here" that could be any here, but that seems to be the term that helps to anchor the spatial coordinates of the scene and so to ground, at least, the spatial ground of its indubitability. When Descartes writes "here," he appears to refer to the place where he is, but this is a term that could refer to any "here" and so fails to anchor Descartes to his place in the way that we might expect it to. What does the writing of his place do to the indubitable referentiality of that "here"? Clearly, it is not here; the "here" works as an indexical that refers only by remaining indifferent to its occasion. Thus, the word, precisely because it can refer promiscuously, introduces an equivocalness and, indeed, dubitability that makes it quite impossible to say whether or not his being "here" is a fact as he claims that it is. Indeed, the very use of such an equivocal term makes it seem possibly untrue.

What I seek to underscore "here," as it were, is that Descartes's very language exceeds the perspective it seeks to affirm, permitting for a narration of himself and a reflexive referentiality that distances the one who narrates from the "I" by whom it is narrated. The emergence of a narrative "I" in the *Meditations* has consequences for the philosophical argument Descartes seeks to make. The written status of the "I" splits the narrator from the very self he seeks to know and *not* to doubt.

The "I" has gotten out of his control by virtue of becoming written. Philosophically, we are asked to accept an "I" who is not the same as the history of its opinions, who can "undo" and "destroy" such opinions and still remain intact. Narratively, we have an "I" that is a textual phenomenon, exceeding the place and time in which it seeks to ground itself, whose very written character depends upon this transposability from context to context.

But things have already become strange, for we were to have started, as Descartes maintains in the "Preface," with reasons, ones that persuade and that give us a clear and distinct idea of what cannot be doubted. We were about to distrust the senses, but instead, we are drawn into the certainties that they provide, the fact that I sit here, am clothed, hold the paper that I am holding, by the fire that is also here.

From this scene, in which indubitability is asserted and withdrawn at once, emerges the question of the body. Descartes asks, "how could I deny that these hands and this body here belong to me?"[6] Consider the very way in which he poses the question, the way in which the question becomes posable within language. The question takes, I believe, a strange grammar, one that affirms the separability of what it seeks to establish as necessarily joined. If one can pose the question whether one's hands and one's body are not one's own, then what has happened such that the question has become posable? In other words, how is it that my hands and my body became something other than me, or at least appeared to be other than me, such that the question could even be posed whether or not they belong to me? What is the status of the question, such that it can postulate a distinction between the "I" who asks and the bodily "me" that it interrogates and so performs grammatically precisely what it seeks to show *cannot* be performed?

Indeed, Descartes begins to ask a set of questions that perform what they claim cannot be performed: "how can I deny that these hands and this body are mine . . ." is one of them, and it is a strange, paralliptical question, because he gives us the graphic contours of such a doubt and so shows that such a doubt is possible. This is, of course, not to say that the doubt is finally sustainable or that no indubitability emerges to put an end to such doubt. For Descartes to claim that the body is the basis of indubitability, as he does, is a strange consequence, if only because it appears to appeal to an empiricism that sustains an uneasy compatibility with the theological project at hand. These examples also seem to relate to the problem of clothing, knowing that one is clothed, for he claims to be sure that he was clothed in his nightgown next to the fire.

The surety of this claim is followed by a series of speculations, however, ones that he imagines that others might make, but that, in his imagining, he himself makes: indeed, the writing becomes the occasion to posit and adopt narrative perspectives on himself that he claims not to be his own, but that, in adopting, are his own in the very mode of their projection and displacement. The other who appears is thus the "I" who, in paranoia, is circuited and deflected through alterity: What of those who think they are clothed in purple, but are really without covering, those others who are like me, who think they are clothed, but whose thinking turns out to be an ungrounded imagining? Descartes, after all, is the one who is actively imagining others as nude, implying, but not pursuing the implication that they might well think of him as nude, as well. But why? Of course, he wants to get beneath the layers that cover the body, but this very occasion of radical exposure toward which the *Meditations* move is precisely what threatens him with an hallucinatory loss of self-certainty.

Indeed, it appears that the certainty he seeks of the body leads him into a proliferation of doubts. He is sure that he sits there clothed: his perspective, as sense perception and not pure intellection, is in that sense clothed or cloaked, thus, this certainty depends on a certain dissimulation. The nudity he attributes to the hallucinatory certainty of others constantly threatens to return to him, to become his own hallucinatory certainty. Indeed, precisely as a sign of radical certainty, that nudity undermines his certainty. If he is clothed, he is certain of what is true, but if he is not, then the truth has been exposed, the body without dissimulation, which leads to the paradoxical conclusion that only if he is deluded about being clothed can his own utterances be taken as indubitable, in which case hallucination and certainty are no longer radically distinguishable from one another.

This is not any nude body, but one that belongs to someone who is deluded about his own nudity, one whom others see in his nudity and his delusion. And this is not simply any "one" with some characterological singularity, but a "one" who is produced precisely by the heuristic of doubt. This is one who calls the reality of his body into question, only to suffer the hallucinatory spectrality of his act. When he sees others in such a state, nude and thinking themselves clothed, he knows them to be deluded, and so if others were to see him in such a state, they would know him to be deluded, as well; thus, the exposure of his body would be the occasion for a loss of self-certainty. Thus, the insistence on the exposed body as an ultimate and indubitable fact in turn exposes the hallucinations of the one who is nude, nude and hallucinating that he or she is fully clothed. This figure of the indubitable body, one that only the mad might doubt, is made to represent the limit case of the res extensa, a body that cannot be doubted, but that, composed of the senses, will be held to be detachable from the soul and its quest for certainty.

If one were to imagine the body instead as an earthenware head or made of glass, as Descartes puts it, one would be doubting what is true. But notice that here, the very act of doubting seems bound up with the possibility of figural substitutions, ones in which the living body is made synonymous with its artifactual simulation or, indeed, with glass, a figure for transparency itself. If the body is certain as *res extensa*, what is to distinguish the human body as *res extensa* from other such instances of substance? If it must, by definition, be separable from the soul, what is to guarantee its humanity? Apparently, nothing can or does.

After all, Descartes not only reports that others perform such hallucinations, the report constitutes the textualization of the

hallucination: his writings perform them for us, through an alienation of perspective that is and is not exclusively his own. Thus, he
conjures such possibilities precisely at the moment in which he also
renounces such possibilities as mad, raising the question whether there
is a difference between the kind of conjuring that is a constitutive part
of the meditative method and those hallucinations that the method is
supposed to refute. He remarks: "I should not be any the less insane
were I to follow examples so extravagant [*si je me reglais sur leurs examples*]." But what if he has already just ruled himself on these examples,
followed these examples, asked us to follow them, in the sense that to
write them is to follow them, and we are clearly following them, as
well, in reading him as we do? The doubt he wants to overcome can
be reenacted only within the treatise, which produces the textual occasion for an identification with those from whom he seeks to differentiate himself. These are his hands, no? But where are the hands that
write the text itself, and is it not the case that they never actually show
themselves as we read the marks that they leave? Can the text ever furnish a certain sense of the hands that write the text, or does the writing eclipse the hands that make it possible, such that the marks on
the page erase the bodily origins from which they apparently emerge,
to emerge as tattered and ontologically suspended remains? Is this not
the predicament of all writing in relation to its bodily origins? There
is no writing without the body, but no body fully appears along with
the writing that it produces. Where is the trace of Descartes's body in
the text? Does it not resurface precisely as the figure of its own dubitability, a writing that must, as it were, make the body strange, if not
hallucinatory, whose condition is an alienation of bodily perspective
in a textual circuitry from which it cannot be delivered or returned?
After all, the text quite literally leaves the authorial body behind, and
yet there one is, on the page, strange to oneself.

At the end of "Meditation I," he resolves to suppose that God is
neither good nor the fountain of truth, but some evil genius, and that

external things are illusions and dreams. Accordingly, he writes, "I shall consider myself as having no hands, no eyes, nor any senses, yet falsely believing myself to possess all these things." It would seem, then, that the task of the meditation is to overcome this doubt in his own body, but it is that doubt that he also seeks to radicalize. After all, it is Descartes's ultimate project to understand himself as a soul, as a *res cogitans*, and not as a body; in this way, he seeks to establish the ultimate dubitability of the body and so to ally himself with those who dream and hallucinate when they take the body to be the basis of certain knowledge. Thus, his effort to establish radical self-certainty as a rational being leads within the text to an identification with the irrational. Indeed, such dreams and hallucinations must be illimitable if he is to understand that certainty of himself as a thinking being will never be furnished by the body.

He writes that "the knowledge of myself does not depend on things not yet known to me." And it does not depend on "things that are *feigned* or *imagined* by my imagination [*celles qui sont feintes et inventées par l'imagination*]."[7] The Latin term—*effingo*—can mean, ambiguously, "to form an image," but also "to make a fact," and this means that his self-knowledge depends neither on forming an image nor making a fact. Inadvertently, Descartes introduces an equivocation between an imagining of what is not a fact and an imagining or making of what is a fact. Has the same imagining wandered across the divide between delusion and reality, such that it is at once what Descartes must exclude as the basis of self-knowledge and what he also must accommodate?

If knowledge does *not* depend on things that are feigned or imagined or facts that are made, then on what does it depend? And does his dismissal of imagining, invention, and factual making not undermine the very procedure of doubt that he uses to gauge the falsifiability of his theses? Indeed, at another moment in the text, he insists that imagination, even invention, serves a cognitive function and that it can be used as the basis for making inferences about the indubitability of

substance itself: "I would invent, in effect, when I am imagining something, since imagining is nothing other than contemplating the figure or image of a corporeal thing."[8]

The imagination is nothing other than the contemplation of the
figure or image of a corporeal thing. The proposition foreshadows the
claims that Husserl will make about the intentionality of the act of
imagining, suggesting that objects appear to the imagination in some
specific modality of their essence. If this is so, then the imagination
does not merely invent bodies, but its inventiveness is also a form of
referentiality, that is, of contemplating the figure or image of bodies
in their essential possibility. The sense in which the imagination is
inventive is not that it produces bodies where there were none. Just as
the referential suggestion of the term *effingo* complicates the problem,
tying imagining to fact making, so Descartes's notion of the image as
relaying the object in some specific way ties imagining to objects of
perception, but in both cases, the link is made not conceptually, but
through a semantic equivocation. Indeed, if the method of doubt involves supposing or positing a set of conditions as true that he then
seeks to doubt, it involves conjecturing what is counterintuitive and
so centrally engages the imagination.

Je supposerai—I suppose, I will suppose, I would suppose—this is
the strange way that Descartes renders his doubt in language, where
the term *supposer* carries the referential ambiguity that plagues his discussion. After all, *supposer* means to take for granted, to accept as a
premise, but also to postulate or posit, to make or to produce. If the
"I" is not a corporeal thing, then it cannot be imagined.

When he writes "I suppose," he offers appositions that suggest its
interchangeability with the following formulations: I persuade myself,
I posit, I think, I believe. The object of that supposing and thinking
takes the form of a different fiction than the one he has just performed:
what he supposes or believes is that "body, figure, extension . . . are nothing but fictions of my own spirit." Here there appears to be going on
a doubling of the fictional, for he is supposing that the body, among

other things, is a fiction of his own mind. But is that supposing not itself a fictionalizing of sorts? If so, is he then producing a fiction in which his body is the creation of a fiction? Does the method not allegorize the very problem of fictive making that he seeks to understand and dispute, and can he understand this fictive making if he continues to ask the question within the terms of the fiction from which he also seeks to escape?

Supposing, self-persuasion, thinking, believing, work by way of positing or, indeed, fabulating—but what is it that is fabulated? If the body is a fiction of one's own spirit, then this suggests that it is made or composed of one's own spirit. Thus, to posit is not merely to conjecture a false world or to make one up, but to invent and refer at the same moment, thus confounding the possibility of a strict distinction between the two. In this way, "the fictions of the spirit" for Descartes are not in opposition to the acts of thinking or persuasion, but are the very means by which they operate. "Positing" is a fiction of the spirit that is not for that reason false or without referentiality. To deny the fictive aspect of positing or supposing is to posit the denial, and in that sense to reiterate the way that the fictive is implicated in the very act of positing. The very means by which Descartes seeks to falsify false belief involves a positing or fictionalizing that, homeopathically, recontracts the very illness it seeks to cure. If the falsification of the untrue must take place though a counterfactual positing, which is itself a form of fiction, then falsification reintroduces fiction at the very moment in which it seeks to refute it. Of course, if we could establish that what is fictional in supposing is not the same as what is fictional in what is being supposed, then we would avoid this contradiction, but Descartes's text does not offer us any way of doing precisely that.

I hope that I have begun to show that in imagining the body, Descartes is at once referring to the body through an image or figure—his words—and also conjuring or inventing that body at the same time and that the terms he uses to describe this act of supposing or imagining carry that important double meaning. Hence, for Descartes, the language in which the body is conjectured does not quite imply that the body is nothing other than an effect of language; it means that conjecturing and supposing have to be understood as fictional exercises that are not devoid of referentiality.

When we consider Descartes's efforts to think the mind apart from the body, we see that he cannot help but use certain bodily figures in describing that mind. The effort to excise the body fails because the body returns, spectrally, as a figural dimension of the text. For instance, Descartes refers to God as one who inscribes or engraves on his soul, when he writes, for instance, that he will never forget to refrain from judgment of what he does not clearly and distinctly understand, "simply by [God's] engraving deeply in my memory the resolution never to form a judgment on" such matters. Descartes's mind is here figured as a slate or a blank page of sorts, and God is figured as an engraver. "God deeply engrave(s) [*gravé*] a resolution in memory not to judge."

Similarly, Descartes appears to imprint a thought on his memory in the same way that God engraves a resolution on the will: he refers to his own human and frail capacity to "forcibly impress [*imprimer*]" a thought on his memory, and so help in the process of building up a new memory where the old one had been destroyed.[9] Meditation now appears as a particular kind of action, one that, he claims, must be repeated and that has as its goal the forcible imprinting (*imprimer*) of this same thought on memory, an imprinting that is as apparently forceful as God's engraving is profound: indeed, both convey a certain formative violence, a rupture of surface, as the effect of writing.

Indeed, "the engraving" is thus the means by which God's will is transferred to Descartes, a peculiar form of transitivity that the trope of writing helps to effect. His memory becomes the object in which God engraves a resolution, as if Descartes's memory were a page, a surface, an extended substance. But this is clearly a problem, since the mind is supposed to be, as we know, *res cogitans*, rather than *res extensa*, whereas it is figured here precisely as an extended surface and substance. Hence, the memory in some ways becomes figured as a kind of body, extended substance and surface, and we might well read here the resurfacing of the lost and repudiated body within the text of Descartes, one on which God now so profoundly engraves a resolution; indeed, the metaphorical stage is now set for Kafka's "In the Penal Colony."

Indeed, it makes sense to ask whether the writing of the *Meditations* is precisely what guarantees this soldering of the memory to the will. The extended writing of the *Meditations* acts to imprint a new knowledge on his memory. To the extent that the page substitutes for memory or becomes the figure through which memory is understood, does that figure then have philosophical consequences, namely, that introspection as method succeeds only to the extent that it is performed in writing on the page? Is writing not precisely the effort to solder a new memory to the will, and if so, does it not require then the very material surface and, indeed, the materiality of language itself that are hardly compatible with what Descartes seeks to separate from the introspective act of the mind? And does this writing not implicitly require the hand of the one who engraves and the body as surface on which to write, dispersing bodily figures throughout the explanation of the soul?

If it seems that Descartes's text cannot but figure the body, that does not reduce the body to its figuration, and if that figuration turns out to be referential, that does not mean that the referent can somehow be extracted from its figuration. The act by which the body is supposed is precisely the act that posits and suspends the ontological status of the body, an act that does not create or form that body unilaterally (and thereby not an act in the service of linguisticism or linguistic monism), but one that posits and figures, one for whom positing and figuring are not finally distinguishable.

If there is no act of positing that does not become implicated in figuration, then it follows that the heuristic of doubt not only entails figuration, but works fundamentally through the figures that compromise its own epistemological aspirations. But this conclusion is immediately impaired by another, namely, that the figuration of the body meets its necessary limit in a materiality that cannot finally be captured by the figure. Here is where proceeding by way of both grammar and figuration falters, though it is a telling faltering. If the body is not reducible to its figuration or, indeed, to its conceptualization, and it cannot be said to be a mere effect of discourse, then what finally is it? The question stands, but just because there is a grammar of the question in which the ontological status of the body is posed does not mean that the answer, if there is one, can be accommodated within the grammatical terms that await that answer. In this case, the posability of the question does not imply its answerability within the terms in which it is posed. The body escapes the terms of the question by which it is approached. And even to make such a formulaic claim, relying on the "the body" as the subject noun of the sentence, domesticates precisely what it seeks to unleash. Indeed, the grammar itself exposes the limits of its own mimetic conceit, asserting a reality that is of necessity distorted through the terms of the assertion, a reality that can appear, as it were, only through distortion.[10]

Descartes makes this point perhaps unwittingly as he proceeds to dismember his own body in the course of his written meditation. We might rush in to say that this "dismemberment" is merely figural, but perhaps, as Paul de Man suggests in another context, it marks the very limits of figuration—its uncanny limits.[11] In reference to Kant, de Man points out that the body in pieces is neither figurative nor literal, but material, thus suggesting that materiality sets the limits to cognition. It follows from his view that the only way to convey that materiality is precisely through catachresis—which is what de Man actually does— and so through a figure.

So is this body figurable or not? It depends, I would suggest, on how one approaches the question of figurality. If Descartes's body is not literally dismembered, though the language figures that as its effect, in what sense is it still dismembered? And if dismemberment is but a sign of a prefigural materiality, then that materiality has been converted into a trope through the very example that is said to illustrate that nonconvertibility. The body does not, then, imply the destruction of figurality, if only because a figure can function as a substitution for what is fundamentally irrecoverable within or by the figure itself.[12] Such a figure is, however, no less a figure than a mimetic one, and a figure need not be mimetic to sustain its status as figural.

Clearly, though, the final question here must be to consider this strange separation of the limbs from the body, this repeated scene of castration, the one that Descartes enacts through the grammar that conditions the question he poses of his body; in which he is already separated from what he calls into question, a separation at the level of grammar that prepares the philosophical question itself; in which the hand that writes the doubt and the hand that is doubted—is it mine?—is at once the hand that is left behind as the writing emerges in, we might say, its dismembering effect.[13]

There is no doubt that a hand writes Descartes's text, a hand figured within that text as appearing at a distance from the one who looks upon it and asks after its reality. The hand is reflexively spectralized in the course of the writing it performs. It undoes its reality precisely at the moment in which it acts, or rather becomes undone precisely by the traces of the act of writing it performs. If the body is what inaugurates the process of its own spectralization through writing, then it is and is not determined by the discourse it produces. If there is a materiality of the body that escapes from the figures it conditions and by which it is corroded and haunted, then this body is neither a surface nor a substance, but the linguistic occasion of the body's separation from itself, one that eludes its capture by the figure it compels.

Merleau-Ponty and the Touch of Malebranche

The English-language reception of Merleau-Ponty's phenomenology of the body focuses mainly on two texts, *Phenomenology of Perception* and the posthumous *The Visible and the Invisible*. In the former, he interrogates the body as a site of mobility and spatiality, arguing that these fundamentally corporeal ways of relating to the world subtend and structure the intentionality of consciousness. In the latter work, the doctrine of intentionality is further displaced by a concept of the flesh, understood as a relation of tactility that precedes and informs inter-subjective relations, necessarily disorienting a subject-centered account. The flesh is not something one has, but, rather the web in which one lives; it is not simply what I touch of the other, or of myself, but the condition of possibility of touch, a tactility that exceeds any given touch and that cannot be reducible to a unilateral action performed by a subject. The most extended and controversial discussion of touch takes place in the final chapter of *The Visible and the Invisible*, "The Intertwining," although that text, posthumously published and unfinished in many ways, can only suggest the radical challenge to a subject-centered conception of intentionality. Something is prior to the subject, but this "something" is not to be understood on the model of a substance. The grammar that would posit a being prior to the subject operates within the presumption that the subject is already formed, merely situated after the being at issue, and so fails to question the very temporality implied by its presentation. What Merleau-Ponty asks in this last work and, indeed, what he began to trace over a decade earlier, is the question how is a subject formed from tactility, or perhaps put more precisely, how is a subject formed by a touch that belongs to no subject?

To speak of a founding touch is no doubt a romantic conceit, and as we will see, it has its theological precedents. To speak in this way makes sense only if we understand that the "touch" in question is not a single act of touching, but the condition by virtue of which a corporeal existence is assumed. Here it would be a mistake to imagine tactility as a subterranean sphere of existence, self-sufficient or continuous through time. The term "tactility" refers to the condition of possibility of touching and being touched, a condition that actively structures what it also makes possible. We cannot locate this condition independently, as if it existed somewhere prior to and apart from the exchange of touch that it makes possible. On the other hand, it is not reducible to the acts of touch that it conditions. How, then, are we to find it? What does it mean that it can be named, but not found, that it eludes our touch, as it were, when we try to lay hold of it? What is it about touch that eludes our touch, that remains out of our reach?

In what follows, I return us to a consideration of Merleau-Ponty's engagement in 1947–48 with the work of Nicolas Malebranche (1638–1715), a set of lectures transcribed by Jean Deprun as *L'union de l'âme et du corps chez Malebranche, Biran et Bergson*.[1] Malebranche was a speculative and theological philosopher whose work on metaphysics and ethics was published in the late seventeenth century. His work had an important effect on Bishop Berkeley and was considered in many ways a serious response to Descartes, one that sought to show the theological and intelligible underpinnings of any account of sentience and sensuousness. Whereas Malebranche embraced a Cartesian view of nature, he sought to rectify Descartes's understanding of mind, arguing that the order of ideal intelligibility is disclosed through sentient experience. Whereas one can have "clear and distinct" ideas of a priori truths, such as mathematical ones, it is not possible to have such clarity and distinctness with respect to one's own self, considered as *a sentiment intérieur*. Against Descartes's argument in the *Meditations* that introspection is the method by which truths of experience may be discerned, Malebranche argued for an experimental, rather than intuitive approach to the idea of our own being. We acquire such a sense of ourselves through time and always with some degree of unclarity and imperfection. This *sentiment intérieur* is occasioned by a divine order that, strictly speaking, cannot be felt; it is derived from an order that remains opaque and irrecoverable. Although Malebranche accepted Descartes's postulation that "I think, therefore I am," he did so for reasons that are at odds with those that Descartes supplies. For Malebranche, the proposition is not a direct inference, but a manifestation of the divine "word" as it makes itself present in experience itself. And although Malebranche separates the "pure" thought of God from its sensuous manifestations, there is no sensuous manifestation that is not derivable from God and that does not, in some way, indicate divine presence and activity. (Only a full and final passivity would withdraw the demonstration of the divine.)

Although in his *The Search after Truth*, Malebranche makes clear that to know what one feels is not the same as knowing what one is,[2] he also argues that sensation offers a demonstration for God, precisely because it cannot, by itself, be the cause of what one feels. That cause comes from elsewhere, and no separate or independent being is its own cause.[3] Although sense experience does not give us adequate knowledge of ourselves or of the order from which we are created (and can lead us astray), it nevertheless indicates that order by virtue of its own enigmatic and partial character. We are caused by God, but not fully determined by him: our actions become "occasions" by which the way we are acted on (by the divine) transforms (or fails to transform) into our own ethical action. The moral life is one that sustains a close relation (*rapport*) with the divine, attempting to establish a mode of human conduct that parallels the divine action by which our conduct is motivated.[4]

Although not a systematic philosopher, Malebranche offered a sustained speculative response to Cartesianism, adapting Augustine to his own purposes and pursuing an empiricism paradoxically grounded in theological premises. The sentiments of the soul could not be dismissed as bodily contaminations, but had to be reconsidered as created experiences that, through their very movement, give some indication—through the presumption of parallelism—of divine origination. Thus, Malebranche disputed the Cartesian distinction between body and soul, arguing not only that the very capacity to feel is inaugurated by an act of "grace," but that sentience itself maintains a referential connection to a spiritual order defined by the incessant activity of self-incarnation.

Merleau-Ponty's considerations in these lectures moved from Malebranche to Maine de Biran and Henri Bergson, reconsidering the relation of the body to thought in each instance and elaborating the contours of a prospective philosophical psychology that insists on the centrality of the body to the act of knowing and on the limits imposed on self-knowledge by the body itself. The notes of these lectures appeared in book form in France in 1978, although they appeared in English only in 2001. One reason, the editors of the English version conjecture, is that these are not precisely Merleau-Ponty's words, although many of them may well be verbatim citations.[5] In addition, Merleau-Ponty is providing an *explication de texte*, but is he offering his own interpretation of the importance of these thinkers to his own philosophy? My suggestion is that he is doing both, deriving resources from the tradition he explicates and, in so doing, disclosing his own relation to the tradition of sensuous theology. It may not at first seem easy to reconcile the focus on embodiment, often conceived as an antidote to forms of religious idealism that postulate a separable "soul," with theological works such as Malebranche's.

In his essay "Everywhere and Nowhere,"[6] Merleau-Ponty situates Malebranche as a precursor of French twentieth-century philosophy, noting that the influential Léon Brunschvieg understood Malebranche, among others, to have established "the possibility of a philosophy that confirms the discordancy between existence and idea (and thus its own unsufficiency)." This Merleau-Ponty compares with the view of Maurice Blondel, "for whom philosophy *was* thought realizing that it cannot 'close the gap,' locating and palpating inside and outside of us a reality whose source is not philosophical awareness."[7] Elaborating on the Christian philosophy bequeathed to contemporary philosophy, Merleau-Ponty makes free with the doctrine to show its promise for his own perspective: "Since it does not take 'essences' as such for the measure of all things, since it does not believe so much in essences as in knots of signification [*nœuds de significations*], which will be unraveled and tied up again in a different way in a new network of knowledge and experience."[8] Merleau-Ponty makes plain that Malebranche not only shows how the religious order, the order of intelligibility, or "the divine Word" intersects with lived experience, indeed, with the senses themselves, but also comes to understand the human subject as the site of this ethically consequential intersection. "If man is really grafted onto the two orders, their connection is also made in him, and he should know something about it. . . . In our view, this is the significance of Malebranche's philosophy. Man cannot be part 'spiritual automaton,' part religious subject who receives the supernatural light. The structures and discontinuities of religious life are met with again in his understanding." He continues, "We are our soul, but we do not have the idea of it; we only have feeling's obscure contact with it" (*le contact obscur du sentiment*). It is in this sense, he writes, that "the slightest sense perception is thus a 'natural revelation.'"[9] The divine does not appear as itself in the sensuous, and neither can the sensuous be said to "participate" in the divine according to a Platonic notion of *mathesis*. Rather, there is a certain division or discordance (*un clivage transversal*) that takes place within sense perception so that its divine origin is obscurely felt, even as it cannot be apprehended.

> It is this very discordancy that one would have to take as one's theme if one wanted to construct a Christian philosophy; it is in it that one would have to look for the articulation of faith and reason. In so doing one would have to draw away from [*s'éloignerait*] Malebranche, but one would also be inspired by him. For although he communicates something of reason's light to religion (and at the limit makes them identical in a single universe of thought), and although he extends the positivity of understanding to religion, he also foreshadows the invasion of our rational being by religious reversals, introducing into it the paradoxical thought of a madness which is wisdom, a scandal which is peace, a gift which is gain.[10]

If an initial skepticism toward the role of Malebranche in Merleau-Ponty's thinking restrains us from considering the usefulness of these lectures, doubt is ameliorated rather quickly, I would argue, when one understands the extent to which Malebranche sought to ground theology in a new conception of the body and, in particular, in the grounding and formative function of touch. Indeed, Malebranche offers Merleau-Ponty the opportunity to consider how the body in its impressionability presupposes a prior set of impressions that act on the body and form the basis for sentience, feeling, cognition, and the beginnings of agency itself. These impressions are, importantly, tactile, suggesting that it is only on the condition that a body is already exposed to something other than itself, something by which it can be affected, that it becomes possible for a sentient self to emerge.

I move too quickly in speaking of a "self" in this regard: a primary impressionability or receptivity forms the condition of experience itself for Malebranche, so that strictly speaking, one does not experience a primary touch, but a primary touch inaugurates experience. This makes of "touch" a speculative notion, to be sure, unverifiable on empirical grounds, that is, on grounds of an "experience" already knowable. In another sense, however, touch reopens the domain of speculation as a necessary precondition for the theorization of embodiment and tactility. This point is made in a different way when we consider that the "tactility" from which touching and being touched both draw is not discernible as a discrete ontological substance of some kind. Another way of putting this is simply to say that touch draws on something it cannot fully know or master. That elusive condition of its own emergence continues to inform each and every touch as its constitutive ineffability. In fact, touch—understood neither simply as touching nor as being touched—not only is the animating condition of sentience, but continues as the actively animating principle of feeling and knowing. What is at least first modeled as a bodily impression turns out to be the condition for cognitive knowing, and in this way, the body comes to animate the soul.

Let me offer a sentence from Malebranche that becomes crucial to Merleau-Ponty's own meditation on the unity of the soul and the body. Malebranche writes, "I can feel only what touches me."[11] Merleau-Ponty cites these words to show that the "I" who feels comes about only consequent to the touch, thus avowing a primacy of the undergoing of touch to the formation of the feeling self. Malebranche's claim is, despite its simplicity and, indeed, its beauty, a quite disarming and consequential claim. First, it postulates the origins of how I come to feel, of what I come to sense, and of sentience itself. Malebranche is claiming that the "I" that I am is one who feels. Although he does not claim here that there is no "I" prior to feeling or apart from feeling, it becomes clear from his argument in favor of the unity of the soul and body that feeling, precipitated by touch, initiates the "I," or rather, institutes its self-representation. After all, what Merleau-Ponty cites from Malebranche is an autobiographical report, which then raises the question, under what conditions does the "I" become capable of reporting on what it feels? We are thus prompted to ask a more fundamental question: Is feeling the condition under which self-reporting in language first takes place? In this citation, offered as a first-person report, feeling does not appear outside of the report on feeling, which suggests that feeling is given form through an autobiographical account. The "I" is not simply a self that comes into being prior to language, but is designated primarily, in the citation at hand, as an act of self-reference within language, a self-reference not only prompted by affect, but animating affect in the act.

If "I" feel only on the condition of being touched, and if feeling is what inaugurates my capacity to report on myself, then it would seem to follow that feeling becomes mine as a distinctly linguistic possibility. But if feeling becomes mine on the condition of an autobiographical report in language, and if feeling follows from a touch that is not mine, then I am, as it were, grounded in, animated by, a touch that I can know only on the condition that I cover over that primary impression as I give an account of myself. "I can feel only what touches me" sets into grammatical form a grammatical impossibility insofar as the touch precedes the possibility of my self-reporting, provides its condition, and constitutes that for which I can give no full or adequate report.

If there can be no "I" without feeling, without sentience, and if the "I" who speaks its feeling is at once the I who feels, then feeling will be part of the intelligible "I," part of what the "I" can and does make intelligible about itself. Indeed, the citation offered us by Merleau-Ponty is an example of the "I" trying to make itself intelligible to itself, considering the prerequisites of its own possibility, and communicating those in language to an audience who, presumably, shares these prerequisites. Yet how would we know whether we do share these prerequisites? The "we" seems ruled out of the scene, and in its place, we listen to another's self-presentation and inhabit the "I" vicariously from a distance. On the one hand, the utterance is an address, delivering a challenge to Descartes and, indeed, to the notion that the "I," the one who speaks and knows, is one who is composed of a thinking substance that is, strictly speaking, distinct from any and all bodily extension—*res cogitans*, rather than *res extensa*.

Yet Malebranche does *not* say, "I can feel only what touches me, and the same goes for you." He is constrained by an autobiographical form that is at once citational, that is, a citation of Descartes, meant to expose the impossibility of Descartes's own position. The markedly citational autobiography gives a partial lie to itself because it is the story of the one who speaks it, and it is at once someone else's story— with a twist. With Descartes, there is something of the threat of so- lipsism, because we do not know if there is a "you" in the scene. "I think, therefore I am" is clearly not the same as "I can feel only what touches me." In neither instance, however, do we know to whom the state- ment is addressed or whether I can report on what another person feels, thinks, or is.

Can I speak of anything that is not mine, that does not become mine by virtue of being my feeling? So there is, we might say, at the beginning of this sentence, a certain scandal, a certain challenge, the one that conjoins the "I" with feeling, the one in which the "I" as- serts itself as a feeling being. And it is not that the "I," on occasion, feels. No, it is rather the case that whatever the "I" will be will be a feeling being. So the "I" is not reporting on this or that stray feeling, but asserting itself on the condition of feeling, which is to say that feeling conditions the "I," and there can be no "I" without feeling. Even though there is a touch that is not mine, it is unclear whether it comes from one who is otherwise like me. It seems not to. The touch is not provided by another self, for Malebranche, and so something in the touch leads us to wonder: Where is the other? If it is the touch of God that animates me, am I then animated only in relation to an irrecoverable and ineffable origin?

If I can feel only what touches me, that means that there is a re- striction on what I can feel. Many consequences follow from this claim: I cannot feel if nothing touches me, and the only thing I can feel is what touches me. I must be touched to feel, and if I am not touched, then I will not feel. If I will not feel, then there is no way to report on what I feel, so there is self-reporting, given that feeling is what appears to animate my entry into linguistic self-representation. Although this last is not a claim that Malebranche explicitly makes, it is an act that he nevertheless performs for us, by (a) asserting the primacy of feeling to what I am and (b) performing the autobiographical account as a consequence of the primacy of feeling. If there is no "I" outside of feeling, and if the "I" makes this case through giving a report on its feeling, then *the narrative "I" becomes the transfer point through which the animated "I" launches an autobiographical construction.* For the "I" is the one who can and does feel, and if there is no touch, there is no "I" who feels, and that means that there is no "I," considered both as the animated effect of feeling and the subject of an autobiographical account. To be touched is, of course, to undergo something that comes from the outside, so I am, quite fundamentally, occasioned by what is outside of me, which I undergo, and this undergoing designates a certain passivity, but not one that is understood as the opposite of "activity." To undergo this touch means that there must be a certain openness to the outside that postpones the plausibility of any claim to self-identity. The "I" is occasioned by alterity, and that occasion persists as its necessary and animating structure. Indeed, if there is to be self-representation, if I am to speak the "I" in language, then this autobiographical reference has been enabled from elsewhere, has undergone what is not itself. Through this undergoing, an "I" has emerged.

Note as well, however, that the sentence implies that I can feel only what touches me, which means that I cannot feel any other thing. No other thing can be felt by me than what touches me. My feeling is prompted, occasioned, inaugurated by its object, and the feeling will be, quite fundamentally, in relation to that object, structured by that object, or, put in phenomenological terms, passively structured in an intentional relation to that object. I do not constitute that object through my feeling, but my capacity to feel and, indeed, therefore to announce myself as an "I" and, thus, to be capable of acting, will follow only on this more fundamental undergoing, this being touched by something, someone. It would appear to follow, as well, that if I cannot be touched, then there is no object, no elsewhere, no outside, and I have become unutterable with the absence of touch. And if I cannot be touched, then there is no feeling, and with no feeling, there is no "I"; the "I" becomes unutterable, something unutterable to itself, unutterable to others. If touch inaugurates a feeling that animates self-representation, and if self-representation can never give a full or adequate account of what animates it, then there is always an opacity to any account of myself I might give. But if there is no touch, there is no account. This is perhaps the difference between a partial account, occasioned by touch, and a radical unaccountability, if not an aphasia, occasioned by a primary destitution.

So what can we conclude so far? That there is in the emergence of the "I," a certain passive constitution from the outside, and that the "I" is borne through feeling, through sentience, and that this sentience is referential: it refers, if only indirectly, to the outside by which it is induced. This would be a passivity prior to the emergence of the "I," a relation that is, strictly speaking, nonnarratable by the "I," who can begin to tell its story only after this inauguration has taken place. Yet can one understand this "passivity," or is this very phrase, and the very grammatical inflexion we use, "being touched," already a fiction retroactively imposed on a condition that is, as it were, before active and passive, that does not, and cannot, know this distinction?

When we consider that for Merleau-Ponty in his late writing "The Intertwining," there will come to be no disposition of being touched that is not at once touching, that the two will be implicated in each other, constituting the *entrelacs* of the flesh itself, how are we to understand this consideration, twelve years earlier, of the constituting condition of the "I"? If being touched precedes and conditions the emergence of the "I," then it will not be an "I" who is touched—no, it will be something before the "I," a state in which touched and touching are obscured by one another, but not reducible to one another, in which distinction becomes next to impossible, but where distinction still holds and where this obscurity, nonnarratable, constitutes the irrecoverable prehistory of the subject. If the touch not only acts on the "I," but animates that "I," providing the condition for its own sentience and the beginnings of agency, then it follows that the "I" is neither exclusively passive nor fully active in relation to that touch. We see that acting on and acting are already intertwined in the very formation of the subject. Moreover, this condition in which passive and active are confounded, a condition, more accurately put, in which the two have not yet become disarticulated, is itself made possible by an animating exteriority. It is not a self-sufficient state of the subject, but one induced by something prior and external. This means that this feeling that follows from being touched is implicitly referential, a situation that, in turn, becomes the basis for the claim that knowing is to be found as an incipient dimension of feeling.

For Merleau-Ponty reading Malebranche, sentience not only preconditions knowing, but gains its certainty of the outside at the very moment that it feels. This sentience is at the outset unknowing about itself; its origin in the passivity of the touch is not knowable. If I feel, there must be an outside and a before to my feeling. My feeling is not a mere given; it is given from somewhere else. Spatial and temporal experience effectively follow from the touch, are induced from the touch retrospectively as its animating conditions. If I feel, then I have been touched, and I have been touched by something outside of myself. Therefore, if I feel, I refer to an outside, but I do not know precisely that to which I refer. Malebranche contends, against Descartes, that "nothing is more certain than an internal sentiment [feeling] to establish knowledge that a thing exists,"[12] but there is no way for sentiment itself to furnish the grounds for the existence of anything; it attests to an existence that is brought into being by an elsewhere, a constitutive alterity. What Malebranche calls "sentiment" is what "alone reveals to us a dimension of the divine life; this profound life of God is only accessible through grace."[13] So we see that grace, understood as the moment of being touched by God and as the rupture that such a touch performs, reveals to us the divine life, where that life is understood, if "understanding" is the word, as an interruption of understanding, a sudden interruption of our time and perspective by that of another. If we stay within the terms of the temporal account that Malebranche offers, however, we would be compelled to say that the rupture, or the interruption, is inaugural; it does not intervene on a preconstituted field, but establishes the field of experience through a traumatic inauguration, that is, in the form of a break, a discordance, or a cleavage of temporalities.

This disorientation within human perspective, however, is not merely occasional. It happens within all thinking. Merleau-Ponty paraphrases Malebranche this way: "No idea is intelligible on its own. It is 'representative of . . .' 'directed toward. . . .'"[14] Thus, every idea is borne, as it were, in and through the sentient relation to an animating alterity. Malebranche, for Merleau-Ponty, therefore anticipates the Husserlian doctrine of intentionality, or so it would seem in light of the language Merleau-Ponty uses to explicate Malebranche's view. Whereas Husserl was always at odds with the *hulê*, the *matter* of the ego and of its objects, Malebranche seems at least occasionally clear that the body offers the formula for ideas, that the body is not discrete time and space, but exists in and as a "secret rapport" with consciousness and so is clearly relational and referential. In this sense, as well, the body carries within it what remains enigmatic to consciousness and so exposes the insufficiency of consciousness: consciousness is *not* a term to which the body corresponds, but the form the body takes when it becomes ideational.

As a result, we should not expect the *cogito* to be discrete and self-knowing. There are, in fact, three parts to the *cogito* as Malebranche understands it: the first is self-knowledge, which is, by definition, obscure; the second is a knowledge of visible ideas of myself, which involves an understanding of myself as a bodily being; and the third is the knowledge of God. The knowledge of God exists in me when I understand the illumination that God provides, an illumination that subsequently informs my ideas, a "light" that is at once a "touch" that God delivers (and, hence, a synesthesia), which gives me my sentience in general and hence my relation to an order of intelligibility. One might be tempted to understand that touch is itself highly figural here, cast as light, emanating from a divinity that, strictly speaking, has no body. It is unclear, as we will see, however, whether the body is abstracted and rendered figural in this account or whether theology is conceding its grounds in a bodily materialism. If there will turn out to be a unity of body and soul in Malebranche, it will not be a simple conjunction of discrete entities, but a dynamic in which ideation follows from tactile impressionability; in this sense, we are working with a theological empiricism of a rather singular kind.

Although ideation follows from the body, bodily experience is not primary. It is animated by what is not fully recoverable through reflective thought. When Malebranche remarks that "I am not the light of myself"[15] and refers to a "created reason," he understands the "I" as necessarily derivative, deprived fundamentally of the possibility of being its own ground. I think, but the referent for my thought transcends the idea that I have, because my idea is never self-sufficient. My idea is derived from and implicitly refers to what is given to me. To the extent that I have ideas, they come to me not merely as gifts, but as miracles, events for which I can give no full account, certainly no causal one. Merleau-Ponty understands Malebranche to be offering a theory of an obscure self-knowledge, obscure, but not for that reason illegitimate. It is obscure precisely because I cannot capture the soul that I am through any idea I may have of it. "I can construct a 'pseudo-idea' of the soul with the notion of extension."[16] Extension will not refer, transparently, to the kind of being that I am. It is not a metaphysical concept that corresponds to a reality, but a necessarily errant metaphor that seeks to capture in conceptual terms what must resist conceptualization itself. In Merleau-Ponty's language, "the soul will remain indeterminate, and the idea we have of it will rest on a half-thought."[17] The soul is not that to which I can have a transparent relation of knowledge: it is partially disclosed, or obscure, precisely because its origins lie elsewhere.

What is the relation between this errant metaphor, this half-thought, and the obscurity that accompanies the originary obscurity of the touch? For Merleau-Ponty, there is in Malebranche an effort to enter deliberately into a *philosophie l'irréfléchi*, a philosophy of the unreflected, of that for which no reflection is possible. Merleau-Ponty writes,

> I am naturally oriented toward my world, ignoring myself. I only know that by experience I can think the past; my memory is not known to me by being seized directly as an operation. My reference to the past is not my work. I receive certain memories that are given to me. I am therefore not a spirit who dominates and deploys time, but a spirit at the disposition of some powers, the nature of which it does not know. I never know what I deserve [*vaux*], whether I am just or unjust. There is a way that I am simply given to myself, and not a principle of myself.[18]

If I am given to myself, but am not a principle of myself, how am I to think this givenness, if I can? As we have already established, it will be a givenness that will never be captured by an idea or a principle, for it will be a nonnarratable and nonconceptualizable givenness (and in this sense *irreflechi*), what I will try to point to with the help of what Merleau-Ponty calls the "entrelacs" or "the intertwining," but where each word will be repelled, indifferently, by what it seeks to name.

What is Merleau-Ponty doing here as he reads and rereads this speculative theology of the late seventeenth century? Merleau-Ponty's enormously provocative final work, *The Visible and the Invisible*, contains within it some of the most beautiful writing we have from him, a writing that not only is about vision and touch, but that seeks, in its own rhythms and openness, to cast language in the mold of the relation he attempts to describe. I would wager that this chapter is the most important work for most feminists, not only because it anticipates what Luce Irigaray will do when she imagines two lips touching (the *deux lèvres* were, in fact, first introduced explicitly in this very chapter by Merleau-Ponty, although tragically lost in the English translation), but because it attempts in a certain way to offer an alternative to the erotics of simple mastery. It makes thinking passionate, because it overcomes, in its language and in its argument, the distinction between a subject who sees and one who is seen, a subject who touches and one who is touched. It does not, however, overcome the distinction by collapsing it. It is not as if everyone is now engaged in the same act or that there is no dynamic and no difference. No, and this is where the distinction between active and passive is confounded, we might say, without being negated in the name of sameness.

This final project of Merleau-Ponty's was dated 1959, two years before he died, and so we see what he was trying to understand more than ten years earlier when he gave his lectures on the speculative theology of Malebranche. Let me state what I think is at stake in this turn, so that my purpose here will not be misunderstood. It is one kind of philosophical contribution to claim that the Sartrian model of the touch or the gaze relies on an untenable subject-object relation and to offer an alternative that shows the way in which the acts of seeing and of being seen, of touching and of being touched, recoil upon one another, imply one another, become chiasmically related to one another. This is a brilliant contribution, one for which Merleau-Ponty is well known. It is another philosophical contribution, however, one attributed to Malebranche, to claim that all knowing is sentient and that sentience has its referential dignity, as it were, that it is a mode of knowing, that it relays the intelligible. By implication, it is a strong and important claim to make that sentience is the ground of all knowing. Yet we are still, in each of these contributions, concerned with a knowing subject, with an epistemological point of departure, with an "I" who is established and whose modes of knowing and feeling and touching and seeing are at issue. How can they be described and redescribed? How can they be accorded a greater philosophical dignity than they have previously enjoyed? Consider that what is happening in the lectures on Malebranche is a different and, I would say, more fundamental philosophical movement, for there the task is *not to provide an account of sentience as the ground of knowing*, but to inquire into the point of departure for sentience itself, the obscurity and priority of its animating condition. So the question is not how to conceive of sentience as the point of departure for knowing, but *how to conceive, if we can, of the point of departure for sentience*. How do we understand, if we can, the emergence of the subject on the condition of touch whose agency cannot fully be known, a touch that comes from elsewhere, nameless and unknowable?

On one hand, this is a theological investigation for Malebranche. It is not only that I cannot feel anything but what touches me, but that I cannot love without first being loved, cannot see without being seen, and that in some fundamental way, the act of seeing and loving are made possible by—and are coextensive with—being seen and being loved. Malebranche writes in *The Search after Truth*, "it might be said that if we do not to some extent see God, we see nothing, just as if we do not love God, i.e. if God were not continuously impressing upon us the love of good in general, we could love nothing."[19] So to love God is to have God continuously impress his love upon us, and so the very moment in which we act, in which we are positioned as subjects of action, is the same moment in which we are undergoing another love, and without this simultaneous and double movement, there can be no love. Love will be the confusion of grammatical position, confounding the very distinction between active and passive disposition. But Malebranche in the hands of Merleau-Ponty—Malebranche, as it were, transformed by the touch of Merleau-Ponty—becomes something different and something more. For here, Merleau-Ponty asks after the conditions by which the subject is animated into being, and although Merleau-Ponty writes of the touch in "The Intertwining," it is unclear whether there is a fundamental inquiry into the animating conditions of human ontology. Was that thought in the background of his writing? Does the confounding of active and passive verb form that follows from the theological inauguration of human sentience in Malebranche not prefigure the chiasm that becomes fundamental to Merleau-Ponty's return to the matter of touch in his posthumous writing? Reading Merleau-Ponty on Malebranche thus resituates the unfinished inquiry that constitutes "The Intertwining," his posthumously published essay, suggesting not only that this inquiry is a local ontology of the touch, but that it offers touch as the name for a more fundamental emergence, the emergence of the "I" on the basis of that chiasm.

To review briefly, then, what is that chiasm? In "The Intertwining," Merleau-Ponty writes,

> the flesh is an ultimate notion . . . it is not the union or compound of two substances, but thinkable by itself, if there is a relation of the visible with itself that traverses me and constitutes me as a seer, this circle which I do not form, which forms me, this coiling over [*enroulement*] of the visible upon the visible, can traverse, animate other bodies as well as my own.[20]

Later, "the flesh we are speaking of is not matter. It is the coiling over of the visible upon the seeing body, of the tangible upon the touching body, which is attested in particular when the body sees itself, touches itself seeing and touching the things, such that, simultaneously, *as* tangible it descends among them."[21]

Already, then, we see that the body is a set of relations, described through a figure, the figure of a coiling or rolling back, and then again, within sentences, as a "fold," anticipating Deleuze. So touched and touching are not reciprocal relations; they do not mirror one another; they do not form a circle or a relation of reciprocity. I am not touched as I touch, and this noncoincidence is essential to me and to touch, but what does it mean? It means that I cannot always separate the being touched from the touching, but neither can they be collapsed into one another. There is no mirror image, and no reflexivity, but a coiling and folding, suggesting that there are moments of contact, of nonconceptualizable proximity, but that this proximity is not an identity, and it knows no closure. At another moment, he calls the flesh "a texture that returns to itself and conforms to itself." This same sentence that I was reading continues. It is a long sentence, and it coils back on itself, refusing to end, touching its own grammatical moments, refusing to let any of them pose as final. Merleau-Ponty thus attempts to end his sentence this way: "*as* touching [the body] dominates them all and draws this relationship and even this double relationship from itself, by dehiscence or fission of its own mass." The flesh is not my flesh or yours, but neither is it some third thing. It is the name for a relation of proximity and of breaking up. If the flesh dominates, it does not dominate like a subject dominates. The flesh is most certainly not a subject, and although our grammar puts it in a subject position, the flesh challenges the grammar by which it is made available to us in language. For whatever reason, the domination that the flesh enacts is achieved through the dehiscence or fission of its own mass. It dominates, in other words, by coming apart: the flesh is what is always coming apart and then back upon itself, but for which no coincidence with itself is possible. So when one touches a living and sentient being, one never touches a mass, for the moment of touch is the one in which something comes apart, mass splits, and the notion of substance does not—cannot—hold. This means that neither the subject who touches nor the one who is touched remains discrete and intact at such a moment: we are not speaking of masses, but of passages, divisions, and proximities. He writes,

> my left hand is always on the verge of touching my right hand touching the things, but I never reach coincidence; the coincidence eclipses at the moment of realization, and one of two things always occurs: either my right hand really passes over to the rank of the touched, but then its hold on the world is interrupted; or it retains its hold on the world, but then I do not really touch *it*—my right hand touching, I palpate with my left hand only its outer covering.[22]

Why would it be the case that my hold on the world is interrupted if the hand by which I seek to touch the world passes over into the rank of the touched? What does it mean to pass over into the rank of the touched? I gather that here Merleau-Ponty is telling us that a pure passivity, understood as an inertness, the inertness of a mass, cannot be the condition of a referential touch, a touch that gives us access to the order of the intelligible. This makes sense, I think, if we reconsider that for Malebranche, to be touched by God is thus to be already, at the moment of the touch, animated into the world and so comported beyond the position of being merely or only touched, being matter, as it were, at the mercy of another, and instead, becoming sentient. I would add the following here, now that we understand the chiasmic relation in which the touch is to be figured: to be touched by God is thus to be made capable of touch, but it would be wrong to say that God's touch precedes the touch of which I become capable. To the extent that I continue to be capable of touching, I am being touched, I am, as it were, having impressed on me the touch of God, and that undergoing is coextensive with the act that I perform. So at the very moment of that ostensible passivity, what we can only call, inadequately, "passivity," what Levinas in a parallel, although not identical move had to call the passivity before passivity, we are activated, but not in such a way that we overcome the passivity by which we are activated: we are acted on and acting at the same instant, and these two dimensions of touch are neither oppositional nor the same. Clearly, we do not, as it were, turn around and touch God in Malebranche's sense, for there is a strict asymmetry in this inaugurative relation, but the asymmetry does not lead to an absolute distinction between touching and being touched. It implies only that they are not the same. So we are, here, in proximity to a relation that is relayed by the middle voice or by a continuous action, but where the acting and the acted on can always and only be figured, but not rigorously conceptualized, where the turn of the one into the other defies conceptualization, makes us grasp for words, leads us into metaphor, error, half-thought, and makes us see and know that whatever words we use at this moment will be *in*adequate and fail to capture that to which they point. Thus, it is not on the basis of our being touched that we come to know the world. It is on the basis of being touched in such a way that touched and touching form a chiasmic and irreducible relation. It is on the basis of this irreducible and nonconceptualizable figure, we might say, that we apprehend the world.

This chiasm, this coiling back, this fold, is the name for the obscure basis of our self-understanding, and the obscure basis of our understanding of everything that is not ourselves. Indeed, there is thus no clarity for me that is not implicated in obscurity, and that obscurity is myself. "If my soul is known through an idea, it must appear to me as a second soul in order to have that idea. It is essential to a consciousness to be obscure to itself if it is to encounter a luminous idea."[23] Here we see that this originary obscurity is the very condition of luminosity. It is not what brings luminosity forth, for the luminous is divine and precedes the emergence of all things human. When we ask after the human access to this light, however, it will be made possible through its own obscurity, a certain dimming against which brightness emerges. To account for this obscurity means accounting for what is given to me, for that by which I am touched, which is irreducibly outside and which, strictly speaking, occasions me. Thus, we arrive at the problem of passivity: "We inherit powers which are not immediately our own. I register the results of an activity with which I am not confused" (*confond*).[24] Thus, my passivity indicates the presence and passion of what is not me and what is situated at the core of who I am as a fundamental scission. We are not far from Levinas at this moment, from the division that not only is fundamental to the subject, but that indicates the operation of alterity in the midst of who I am.

For Merleau-Ponty, following Malebranche, no unity resolves the tension of this internal relation, and this relation is not supported by a common space or a common shelter named the subject. Indeed, the relation finds itself in a disunity with no promise of reconciliation. This is an inevitable "scission" in a philosophy where there must be a detour for going from the self to itself, a passage through alterity that makes any and all contact of the soul with itself necessarily obscure. This obscurity is lived not only as passivity, but, more specifically, as feeling, a sentiment of the self. This interior sense of myself—obscure, passive, feeling—is the way that God is, as it were, manifest in the human soul. It is by virtue of this connection, which I cannot fully know, between sentience and God, that I understand myself to be a free being, one whose actions are not fully determined in advance, for whom action appears as a certain vacillating prospect. The interior sense of freedom is the power that a man has to follow or not follow the way that leads to God. In fact, the interior sense of myself is sufficient to reaffirm my freedom, but this same sense of myself is insufficient to know it.[25]

Indeed, there is no inspection of myself that will furnish any clear access to intelligibility, for that inspection of myself will of necessity refer me elsewhere, outside. For there to be an illumination that is necessary for understanding, indeed, in Merleau-Ponty's reading, "for there to be light, there must be, facing me, a *representative being* . . . otherwise, my soul will be dispersed and at the mercy of its states."[26] So a subject who has only its own feeling to rely on, whose feeling is given no face, encountered by a representative of "being," is one who suffers its own dispersion, living at the mercy of its own random feeling. What holds those states and feelings together is not a unity to be found at the level of the subject, but one only conferred by the object in its ideality. It is the one addressed by such feeling who confers intelligibility on one's own desire. This other, the one to whom feeling is addressed, the one who solicits feeling, does so precisely to the extent that the Other represents being. For that Other to represent being is not for it to be being itself, but to be its sign, its relay, its occasion, its deflection.

The human heart is empty and transient without this being. To say, then, that sentience is referential in this context is to say, with

Merleau-Ponty, that "there must be a being . . . which refers to reality, because the human soul is not by itself this agility and this transparence which alone is capable of knowledge."[27] So whatever this referent is will not be the same as its representative, and this means, for Malebranche, that God is not the same as his objects. For Merleau-Ponty, this claim is cast in such a way that one can see its resonance with the phenomenological claim that there is an ideal point according to which variations in perspectives become possible and that the beings we come to know are the various perspectives of that ideal. In a sense, Malebranche prefigures in his description of God as the one who "sees" and endows all things with his perspective the conception of the noematic nucleus for phenomenology. This gives Merleau-Ponty a way to distinguish the order of intelligibility from the order of its signification. The "intelligible extension" that characterizes various kinds of beings is, significantly, "not close to the subject (it is not a fact of knowledge), nor is it close to the object (it is not an in-itself). It is the ideal kernel according to which real extension [substance] is offered to knowledge."[28] Thus, what one feels, if it is a feeling, if it is a sense, if it is love, or even if it is a touch, for instance, is sustained by the ideality of its addressee, of the uncapturability of the referent, the irreducibility of the ideal to any of its perspectival adumbrations.

So when Merleau-Ponty writes of Malebranche that "he does not conceive of consciousness as closed, its meanings are not its own,"[29] he means to show how this consciousness is given over from the start, prior to any decision to give itself over, prior to the emergence of a reflexive relation by which it might, of its own accord, give itself over. It is given over to an infinity that cannot be properly conceptualized and that marks the limits of conceptualization itself. "A property of infinity that I find incomprehensible," writes Malebranche, "is how the divine verb hides [*renferme*] the body of its intelligible mode."[30] The divine verb, the linguistic action that the divine takes, is not made known in a verb that might be understood. No, that verb is hidden, shut up, concealed, *renfermer*, offered in an enigmatic fashion, unreadable within the grammar that we know. In the terms of conventional language, the verb is unintelligible, but its unintelligibility, from the human perspective, is a sign of the divine intelligibility it encloses. The divine verb renders the body enigmatic precisely as a way to enter the body into the intelligible mode: "*le Verbe divin renferme les corps d'une manière intelligible.*" So the verb wraps that body up in an intelligible mode, but what of the body exceeds that wrapping? And the divine verb, which is it? We are given the verb for what the divine verb does, although this is not, we must suppose, the divine verb itself. The word we are given is *renfermer*: to shut or lock up; to enclose, to contain, to include. *Renfermer* stands for the divine verb, and we might even say that it is the verb "*qui renferme le Verbe divin,*" the one that has that divine verb enigmatically contained within it, where what is contained—and so not contained at all—is "an incomprehensible thought of infinity."

This enigmatic infinity, however, pertains to bodies and to how they are included within the realm of intelligibility. There is something enigmatic there and something infinite, something whose beginning we cannot find, something that is resistant to narrativization. It is difficult to know how the divine is instantiated in bodies, but also how bodies come to participate in the divine. Through what enigmatic passage do bodies pass such that they attain a certain ideality, such that they become, as it were, a representative of an ideality that is inexhaustible, infinite, something about which I could not give an account, for which no account would finally suffice??

In the edition of the lectures from 1947–48 that I have cited here, an appendix is included called "*Les sens et l'inconscient*" (The senses and the unconscious), a brief lecture that Merleau-Ponty delivered in this same academic year, but that was not formally linked to the lectures collected in the book. One can see at a glance why it is included, why it should be.[31] Merleau-Ponty writes, "the unconscious . . . is nothing but a call to intelligence to which intelligence does not respond, because intelligence is of another order. There is nothing to explain outside of intelligence, and there is nothing to explain here, but only something that asserts itself, simply."[32] Here, Merleau-Ponty makes clear the sense of the "unconscious" that he accepts, and it has to do with the way in which the unknown, and the unknowable, pervades the horizon of consciousness. In this sense, he is concerned, as was Malebranche, with how an order of intelligibility that is not fully recoverable by consciousness makes itself known, partially and enigmatically, at the level of corporeity and affect. In his view, it would be a mistake to claim, for instance, that when I fall in love, and am conscious of every phase of feeling I go through, I therefore understand something of the form and significance that each of these lucid images has for me, how they work together, what enigma of intelligibility they offer up. It is necessary, he writes, to distinguish between being in love and knowing that one is in love. "The fact that I am in love is a reason not to know that I am, because I dispose myself to live that love instead of placing it before my eyes."[33] Even if I attempt to see it, Merleau-Ponty insists, "My eyes, my vision, which appears to me as prepersonal . . . my field of vision is limited, but in a manner that is imprecise and variable . . . my vision is not an operation of which I am the master."[34] Something sees through me as I see. I see with a seeing that is not mine alone. I see, and as I see, the I that I am is put at risk, discovers its derivation from what is permanently enigmatic to itself.

That our origins are permanently enigmatic to us and that this enigma forms the condition of our self-understanding clearly resonate with the Malebranchian notion that self-understanding is grounded in a necessary obscurity. What follows is that we should not think that we will be able to grasp ourselves or, indeed, any object of knowledge, without a certain failure of understanding, one that makes the grasping hand, the figure for so much philosophical apprehension, a derivative deformation of originary touch. If we think we might return to an originary touch, however, and consult it as a model, we are doubtless radically mistaken. For what is original is precisely what is irrecoverable, and so one is left with a pervasive sense of humility when one seeks to apprehend this origin, a humility that gives the lie to the project of mastery that underlies the figure of the mind "grasping" its origins. "An analysis should be possible," Merleau-Ponty writes, "which defines thought not by the plenitude by which it seizes its object, but by the sort of stopping of the activity of spirit which constitutes certitudes, one which subjects these certitudes to revision, without reducing them to nothing. It is necessary to introduce a principle of thought's lack of adequation to itself."[35] It is not that thought is lacking something, but that we are lacking in relation to the entire field of intelligibility within which we operate. We cannot know it fully, even as it gives us our capacity to know.

The point here is not to reduce Merleau-Ponty's phenomenology of touch to a psychoanalytic perspective, but perhaps to suggest that Merleau-Ponty recasts psychoanalysis as a seventeenth-century theology, bringing both together in a tactile revision of phenomenology. "It must be possible," he claims, "to "recognize the origin of a principle of passivity in freedom." The passivity to which he refers is a kind of primary undergoing for which we have always and only an obscure and partial knowledge. To recognize the origin of a principle of passivity in freedom is not to understand passivity as derived from freedom, but to understand a certain passivity as the condition of freedom, supplying a limit for the model of freedom as self-generated activity.

What follows is that whatever action we may be capable of is an action that is, as it were, already underway, not only or fully our action, but an action that is upon us already as we assume something called action in our name and for ourselves. Something is already underway by the time we act, and we cannot act without, in some sense, being acted upon. This acting that is upon us constitutes a realm of primary impressionability so that by the time we act, we enter into the action, we resume it in our name, it is an action that has its source only partially and belatedly in something called a subject. This action that is not fully derived from a subject exceeds any claim one might make to "own" it or to give an account of oneself. Yet our inability to ground ourselves is based on the fact that we are animated by others into whose hands we are born and, hopefully, sustained. We are thus always, in some way, done to as we are doing, that we are undergoing as we act, that we are, as Merleau-Ponty insisted, touched, invariably, in the act of touching. Of course, it is quite possible to position oneself so that one might consider oneself only touched, or only touching, and pursue positions of mastery or self-loss that try to do away with this intertwining, but such pursuits are always partially foiled or struggle constantly against being foiled. Similarly, it may well be that some humans are born into destitution and fail to become human by virtue of being physically deprived or physically injured, so there is no inevitability attached to becoming animated by a prior and external touch. The material needs of infancy are not quite the same as the scene that Malebranche outlines for us as the primary touch of the divine, but we can see that his theology gives us a way to consider not only the primary conditions for human emergence, but the requirement for alterity, the satisfaction of which paves the way for the emergence of the human itself. This does not mean that we are all touched well or that we know how to touch in return, but only that our very capacity to feel and our emergence as knowing and acting beings is at stake in the exchange.

The Desire to Live

Spinoza's Ethics *under Pressure*

The desire to live is not an easy topic to pursue. On the one hand, it seems too basic to thematize; on the other hand, it is vexed enough as a topic to cast doubt on whether one can settle the question of what is meant by the phrase itself. The desire to live is not the same as self-preservation, though both can be understood as interpretations of a person's desire "to persevere in its being,"[1] Spinoza's well-known phrase. Although self-preservation is largely associated with forms of individual self-interest associated with later contractarian political philosophers, Spinoza's philosophy establishes another basis for ethics, one that has implications for social solidarity and a critique of individualism. The self that endeavors to persevere in its own being is not always a singular self for Spinoza, and neither does it necessarily succeed in augmenting or enhancing its life if it does not at once enhance the lives of others. Indeed, in what follows, I hope to establish within Spinoza not only a critical perspective on individualism, but also an acknowledgment of the possibility for self-destruction. Both of these insights come to have political implications when recast as part of a dynamic conception of political solidarity in which sameness cannot be assumed. The fact that Spinoza takes some version of self-preservation to be essential to his conception of human beings is undisputed, but what that self is and what precisely it preserves is less than clear. He has been criticized by psychoanalysts who contend that he leaves no room for the death drive, and he has been appropriated by Deleuzians who for the most part wish to root negativity out of their conception of individuality and sociality alike. He has been castigated, as well, by writers like Levinas for espousing a form of individualism that would eradicate ethical relationality itself. I propose to test these views and to consider in some detail Spinoza's view of the desire to live—not to establish a definitive reading, but to see what possibilities for social ethics emerge from his view.

When Spinoza claims that a human being seeks to persevere in its own being, does he assume that the desire to live is a form of self-preservation? Moreover, what conceptions of the "self" and of "life" are presupposed by this view? Spinoza writes, "The striving by which each thing strives to persevere in its being is nothing but the actual essence of the thing" (IIIP7, 159). It would seem that whatever else a being may be doing, it is persevering in its own being, and at first, this seemed to mean that even various acts of apparent self-destruction have something persistent and at least potentially life-affirming in them. I've since come to question this idea, and part of the purpose of this essay will be to query what, if anything, counters the force of perseverance itself. The formulation is problematic for another reason, as well, since it is not fully clear in what "one's own being" consists, that is, where and when one's own being starts and stops. In Spinoza's *Ethics*, a conscious and persevering being does not persevere in its own being in a purely or exclusively self-referential way; this being is fundamentally responsive, and in emotional ways, suggesting that implicit in the very practice of perseverance is a referential movement toward the world. Depending on what kind of response a being undergoes,

that being stands a chance of diminishing or enhancing its own possibility of future perseverance and life. This being desires not only to
persevere in *its own* being, but to live in a world that reflects and furthers the possibility of that perseverance; indeed, perseverance in one's
own being requires that reflection from the world, such that persevering and modulating reference to the world are bound up together.
Finally, although it may seem that the desire to persevere is an individual desire, it turns out to require and acquire a sociality that is essential
to what perseverance means; "to persevere in one's own being" is thus
to live in a world that not only reflects but furthers the value of others'
lives as well as one's own.

In the fourth part of the *Ethics*, entitled "Of Human Bondage, *or*
The Powers of the Affects," Spinoza writes, "No one can desire to be
blessed, to act well and to live well, unless at the same time he desire
to be, to act, and to live, that is, to actually exist" (IVP21, 211). The
desire to live well presupposes the desire to live, or so he suggests. To
persevere in one's own being is to persevere in life and to have self-
preservation as an aim. The category of life seems, however, to tra-
verse both what is "one's own" and what is clearly not only or merely
one's own. The self preserved is not a monadic entity, and the life
persevered in is not only to be understood as a singular or bounded
life. Importantly, in the disposition toward others, where the self makes
its encounter with another, the *conatus* is enhanced or diminished, so
that it is not possible, strictly speaking, to refer to *one's own* power without referring to and responding to other powers—that is, the powers
that belong to others. Similarly, it is not possible to refer to one's own
singularity without understanding the way in which that singularity
becomes implicated in the singularities of others, where, as we will
see, this being implicated produces a mode of being beyond singularity
itself.

For Spinoza, self-preservation is enhanced or diminished depending on the way in which others appear; they arrive physically, and
they wield the power of reflection. More precisely, they reflect back

something about life itself, and they do this in variable ways. Much of the second part of the *Ethics* is devoted to lists of these kinds of experiences. The *conatus* is augmented or diminished depending on whether one feels hatred or love, whether one lives with those with whom agreement is possible, or whether one lives with those with whom agreement is difficult, if not impossible. It seems that self-preservation is, in nearly every instance, bound up with the question of what one feels toward another or how one is acted on by another. If we are to call this being that one is a "self," then it would be possible to say that the self represents itself to itself, is represented by others, and that in this complex interplay of reflection, life is variably augmented or diminished. Actually, what the self does, constantly, is imagine what a body would do or does do, and this imagining becomes essential to its relation to others. These imaginary conjectures are not simple reflections, but actions of a certain kind, the expression of *potentia*, and, in that sense, expressions of life itself. *This means that the way that we represent others to ourselves or the means by which we are represented to ourselves by or through others constitute expressive actions by which life itself is augmented or diminished.* In representing others as we do, we are positing possibilities and imagining their realization. Life stands the chance of becoming enhanced through that process by which the *potentia* of life are expressed.

If we are to understand this formulation, one that Deleuze clearly facilitated in his early readings of Spinoza,[2] we have to become disoriented by the formulation itself. For it turns out that to persevere in one's own being means that one cannot persevere in that being understood as radically singular and set apart from a common life. To be set apart from the interplay of selves and their reflective powers is to be deprived of the representational and expressive apparatus by which life itself is enhanced or diminished. Indeed, the very meaning of the life that is, finally, one's own to persevere in becomes equivocal in this formulation. So if we are to speak about desiring to live, it would seem in the first instance to be emphatically a personal desire, one that pertains to my life or to yours. It will turn out, however, that to live means to participate in life, and life itself will be a term that equivocates between the "me" and the "you," taking up both of us in its sweep and dispersion. Desiring life produces an *ek-stasis* in the midst of desire, a dependence on an externalization, something that is palpably not me, without which no perseverance is possible. What this means is that I start out with a desire for life, but this life that I desire puts the singularity of this "I" into question. Indeed, no I can emerge outside of this particular matrix of desire. So, strictly speaking, one should say that *in desiring, I start out—that desire starts me as an "I"—and that the force of desire, when it is the desire to live, renders this "I" equivocal.* Accordingly, the *Ethics* does not and cannot remain with the question of individual perseverance and survival, since it turns out that the means by which self-preservation occurs is precisely through a reflection or expression that not only binds the individual to others, but expresses that bind as already there, as a bind in several senses: a tie, a tension, or a knot, something from which one cannot get free, something constitutive that holds one together. So on the one hand, the problematic of life binds us to others in ways that turn out to be constitutive of who each of us singly is. On the other hand, that singularity is never fully subsumed by that vexed form of sociality; for Spinoza, the body establishes a singularity that cannot be relinquished in the name of a greater totality, whether it be a conception of a common life or a political understanding of *civitas*, or, indeed, of the multitude (*multitudo*), a term that becomes important, very briefly, in Spinoza's *A Theologico-Political Treatise*, a work that remained incomplete at his death.

I will return to the question of this relation between singularity and commonality in a later section of this essay, especially when I consider the criticism that Levinas has made of Spinoza, but let us first return to the other quotation from Spinoza with which I began. At first, it seems to be relatively straightforward, namely, that "no one can desire to live well, unless at the same time he desires to be, to act, and to live." It appears that the meaning of this line is to be understood in the following way: the desire to live well calls upon the desire to be and to live, and that this latter desire to live must first be in place for the desire to live well to come into play. According to this view, the desire to live well is a way of qualifying the prior desire to live, and living well is but a permutation of living. This reading is thwarted, however, because Spinoza does not quite say that the desire to live well presupposes the desire to live. He writes that both desires are engaged simultaneously. They both emerge "at the same time." It is as if in desiring to live well one finds that one has engaged the desire to live. Or perhaps one encounters only belatedly the desire to live, only after it makes itself known as the unacknowledged underside of the desire to live well. This formulation also leaves open the possibility that living in the wrong way can induce the desire not to live, or, indeed, diminish the organism in Spinoza's sense. This seems to be the sense of what he is maintaining when he makes the following kind of claim: "Envy is hatred itself or sadness, that is, a modification by which a man's power of acting or endeavour (persistence) is hindered."

Spinoza's is a controversial claim, if he is claiming, as he appears to be, that the virtuous life works *with*, rather than against, the desire to live. Of course, it may be that the desire to live is a necessary precondition for the desire to live well, and that it also undergirds the desire to live wrongly, and that the desire to live is finally in itself neutral with respect to the question of living rightly or wrongly. But even this last, minimal interpretation leaves untouched the question of whether living rightly might sometimes entail a restriction on the desire to live itself. There is no repressive law that attacks some life force, whether that life force is conceived as the Nietzschean will to power or the Freudian conception of libidinal drives. And there is no sense that the right life might demand that we enfeeble ourselves in the name of morality, as Nietzsche and Freud have both suggested. The account Freud gives in *Civilization and Its Discontents* (1927), namely, that living well can come at a cost to the life drives themselves, is not anticipated in Spinoza's ethical reflections. One can argue in a psychoanalytic vein that the desire to live the right sort of life can compromise the desire to live and that morality requires the activation of a suicidal tendency. This would seem to be in contradiction to Spinoza's explicit views. Indeed, he rejects the notion that anyone might commit suicide "from the necessity of his own nature" and suggests that suicidal desires can be "compelled" only "by another" (IVP20S, 210–11). Of course, Spinoza distinguishes between forms of pleasure that diminish the desire to live and those that enhance or augment that desire, so he locates the possibility of an attrition of life that is achievable through pleasure and passion more generally. He also links the emotions to human bondage; there is the possibility of passivity and servitude in passion, which, for him, undermine the possibility of both persevering in the desire to live and living virtuously.

That said, however, Spinoza disputes that the desire not to exist can actually be derived from human desire, something he has already and consistently defined as the desire to persevere in one's own being. When he imagines how suicide might be conducted, he writes, "Someone may kill himself if he is compelled by another, who twists his right hand (which happens to be holding a sword)" (IVP20S, 210–11). He also cites the example from Seneca in which a suicide is coerced by a tyrant as a form of obligated political action. The third conjecture he offers is enigmatic, since it promises an analysis it does not pursue. There, Spinoza suggests that a man may commit suicide "because hidden external causes [*causae latentes externae*] so dispose his imagination, and so affect his body, that it takes on another nature" (IVP20S, 211). This is surely a paradoxical claim, since Spinoza acknowledges that a suicide can take place, that the self can take its own life, but that the self has acquired an external form, or, indeed, an external cause has made its way into the structure of the self. This allows him to continue to argue that a person takes his own life only by virtue of external causes, but not by any tendency internal to human desire itself, bound to life as it ostensibly is.

This external cause that houses itself in the self is something for which I cannot have an "idea" and is thus an unconscious sort of operation, one that I cannot understand as proper to myself, something that is for me an object, or, indeed, an external intrusion. The I is said to have taken on or contracted this externality, and so it has absorbed it through some means for which it has no representation and can have no representation. Indeed, the I becomes something other to itself in taking in this externality; it becomes, quite frankly, other to itself: obdurate, external, hidden, a cause for which no idea suffices.

At this point, it may be that Spinoza himself has admitted something into his theory that threatens the consistency of his account of desire and that he has momentarily assumed the form of some other conception of desire, one that would orient it against life. And though I think here we can see a certain prefiguration of the death drive— one invoked in the commentary on the proposition, only to be disposed of quite quickly—I would suggest that there are ways to see Spinoza's unsettled relation to a psychoanalysis he could have never anticipated. There is already, apart from his introduction of this hidden external cause in the life of desire, a manner in which externality works upon desire that modulates its relation to life. I hope to show some of this in what follows and to suggest that his view, however improbable it may seem in the light of contemporary thinking on the drives or desire in general, prefigures some of the continuing difficulties that beset these discussions.

Spinoza's ethics does not supply a set of prescriptions, but offers an account of how certain dispositions either express or fail to express the essence of humankind as the desire to persevere in one's being. The phrase "each thing strives to persevere in its being" functions as a description of human ontology, but also as an exhortation and an aspiration. It is not a morality in a conventional sense if, by morality, we mean a more or less codified set of norms that govern action. But if, for Spinoza, any morality is to be called virtue and we understand virtue, the virtuous life, as governed by reason, as he claims we must, then it follows that the *conatus* will be enhanced by the virtuous life, and there will be no cost to life, properly understood, if we live well.

Psychoanalysis approaches this question from another angle, since self-preservation comes to represent one of the basic drives for Freud, and this is so from nearly the beginning of his writings. But self-preservation is a drive that is eventually supplemented and countered by the death drive. This has consequences for the way in which Freud thinks about morality. Indeed, conscience harnesses the death drive to a certain degree, so that morality is always cutting away at the life drives. For Freud, it would seem that sometimes the dictates of morality require that self-preservation be suspended or put into question. And in this sense, morality can be murderous, if not suicidal. For Spinoza, however, self-preservation, understood as perseverance or endeavoring in one's desire, provides the basis for virtue, or living well, and he assumes further that living well enhances life and the capacity for perseverance in it. Not only does the desire to live well presuppose the desire to live, it follows that suicidal persons are at risk for some rather bad behavior. For Spinoza, living well might relieve the diminishing sense of life that is a kind of slow suicide.

Such ethical optimism is not only countered by Freud's account of the drives, but from a different direction, by Levinas's conception of ethics. For Levinas, self-preservation cannot be the basis of ethics, which is not to say that self-annihilation should take its place. Both relations are problematic, because they set up a relation to the self as prior to the relation to the other. It is this latter relation that forms the basis of ethics, in his view. I would like first to conjecture the psychoanalytic rejoinder to Spinoza and then turn to Levinas in order to understand why he explicitly faults Spinoza for positing self-preservation as a precondition of virtuous conduct. For Levinas, it will turn out, there is no "other" for Spinoza, but only and always the self. But it may be that in reapproaching Spinoza through the lens of psychoanalysis, we find a way of adjudicating this quarrel about just how much violence we are compelled to do to ourselves and, indeed, to others, in the name of morality.

Freud's thesis in *Civilization and its Discontents* is that morality, centralized and institutionalized as conscience, demands a renunciation of the life drive. Indeed, the very process by which conscience is formed is the process through which a renunciation and transformation of drive into conscience takes place. In this text, he recounts his argument from *Beyond the Pleasure Principle* (1920), in which he distinguishes self-preserving instincts, or more rightly, drives (*Triebe*), from the death drive. He writes:

> Starting from speculations on the beginning of life and from biological parallels, I drew the conclusion that, besides the instinct to preserve living substance and to join it into ever larger units, there must exist another, contrary instinct seeking to dissolve those units and to bring them back to their primaeval, inorganic state. That is to say, as well as Eros there was an instinct of death. . . . The manifestations of Eros were conspicuous and noisy enough. It might be assumed that the death instinct operated silently within the organism towards its dissolution, but that, of course, was no proof. A more fruitful idea was that a portion of the instinct is diverted towards the external world and comes to light as an instinct of aggressiveness and destructiveness.[3]

Freud makes two claims about life in the course of his discussion of the death drive that are not precisely compatible with one another. On the one hand, he distinguishes life drives from death drives and claims, in sweeping terms, "the meaning of the evolution of civilization is no longer obscure to us. It must present the struggle between Eros and Death, between the instinct of life and the instinct of destruction, as it works itself out in the human species."[4] But immediately after this statement, he suggests that the struggle itself *is* life and that life is not reducible to the life drive. He states, "This struggle is what all life essentially consists of, and the evolution of civilization may therefore be simply described as the struggle for life of the human species."[5] The struggle he refers to is a struggle *between* the two drives, one of which is the life drive, but it is also a struggle *for life*, implying that life is a struggle composed of the interplay of both the life and death drives. Life itself seems to be a term that switches between these two meanings, exceeding its basis in the drives, we might say, through a displacement that ceaselessly accommodates its apparent opposite. Indeed, one reason to use the term "drive," rather than "instinct," is that the notion of the "drive" is, as Freud argues, a border concept, vacillating between the domains of somatic and mental representation.[6] In Freud's text, the drive does not stay still (as Laplanche points out in his *Life and Death in Psychoanalysis*).[7] The struggle for life is not the same as the simple operation of the life drive; whatever "life" is said to adhere to, that drive alone is not the same as life, understood as an ongoing struggle. There is no struggle, and hence, no life, without the death drive (*Todestrieb*). In that sense, without the death drive, there is no struggle for life. If life itself *is* this struggle, then there is no life without the death drive. We can even extrapolate logically that life without the struggle provided by the death drive would itself be death. Such a life would be no life, and so, paradoxically, the triumph of the death drive over life.

So it would seem that life requires the death drive in order to be the struggle that it is. Life requires the death drive, but it also requires that the death drive not triumph. But it would also appear that the death drive plays a specific role in the emergence and maintenance of morality, especially the workings of conscience. For Freud, morality runs the risk of cutting away at life itself.

In "Mourning and Melancholia" (1914), Freud relates that the suffering of the melancholic is enigmatic: the melancholic suffers from loss, but does not know precisely what he or she has lost. The clinician sees the melancholic absorbed in something and also losing self-esteem. One may know that one has lost someone or some object, but one cannot seem to find "what" is lost in the one who is lost or "what" kind of ideal is lost when, say, historical circumstance shifts a political formation, demands a geographical displacement, or introduces uncertainty into the very conception of where one belongs or how one may name oneself. One cannot quite see it, but it makes itself known nevertheless; the loss appears in a deflected form, as the diminution of self-esteem and in the escalation of self-beratement. In mourning, Freud tells us famously, the world becomes impoverished, but in melancholia, it is the ego itself. The ego does not simply find itself impoverished, shorn of some esteem it once enjoyed, but the ego begins, as if inhabited by an external cause, to strip away its self-esteem. Freud describes it as a violent act of self-reproach, finding oneself morally despicable, vilifying and chastising oneself. In fact, this loss of self-esteem can lead to suicide, because, according to Freud, the process of unchecked melancholia can conclude with "an overthrow, psychologically very remarkable, of that drive that constrains every living thing to cling to life."[8]

Whereas mourning seems to be about the loss of an object—the conscious loss of an object—melancholics do not know what they grieve. And they also somewhere resist the knowledge of this loss. As a result, they suffer the loss as a loss of consciousness and so of a knowing self. To the degree that this knowing secures the self, the self is also lost, and melancholy becomes a slow dying away, a potentially suicidal attrition. This attrition takes place through self-beratement and self-criticism, and can take the form of suicide, that is, attempting to obliterate one's own life on the basis of its own felt contemptuousness.

Freud returns to this theme in his essay "The Economic Problem of Masochism" (1924), in which he attempts to spell out the phenomenon of moral masochism and understand its role in giving evidence for the death drive. In moral masochism, he claims, we see the least amount of pleasure at work for the psychic organism; it is unclear whether there is pleasure at all in this state. This form of masochism does not draw upon the resources of pleasure, or, indeed, the life drive, and also risks devolving into suicide. The death drive, left alone, will attempt to "disintegrate the cellular organism,"[9] he writes, and so functions as a principle that *de*constitutes the ego. Although Freud generally understands sadism as an outwardly directed act of aggression accompanied by the life drive, masochism of the moral kind not only turns aggression against the self, but dissociates it from pleasure and hence from life, thereby imperiling the very perseverance of the organism.

This leads Freud to conclude that masochism is a primary expression of the death drive and that sadism would be its derivative form, a form that mixes the death drive with pleasure and, so, with life. He writes, spectacularly, that "it may be said that the death drive which is operative in the organism—primal sadism—is identical with masochism."[10] Moral masochism, "loosened" from sexuality, seeks suffering and derives no gain from the suffering. Freud postulates that an unconscious sense of guilt is at work here, a sense of guilt that seeks "satisfaction," not, however, a satisfaction of pleasure, but rather an expiation of guilt and the death of pleasure itself. Freud explains: "The super-ego—the conscience at work in the ego—may then become harsh, cruel and inexorable against the ego which is in its charge. Significantly, conscience and morality have arisen through the desexualization of the Oedipus Complex, and suicide becomes a temptation precisely when this desexualization becomes complete."[11]

Moral masochism approaches suicide, but to the extent that self-beratement is eroticized, it maintains the organism it seeks to decompose. Oddly, in this sense, morality works against the libido, but can marshal the libido for its own ends and so keep the struggle between life and death alive. In Freud's words, "through moral masochism, morality becomes sexualized once more."[12] Only when morality ceases to make use of libido does it become explicitly suicidal. Of course, we may want to question this claim and remind ourselves of that final moment in Kafka's "Judgment," when the apparent murder / suicide of Georg, who hurls himself from that bridge, is likened, by Kafka in his journals, to ejaculation itself.

So for Freud, morality, which is not the same as ethics, makes use of the death drive; by virtue of becoming sexualized as masochism, it animates the desire to live, as well. Morality would have to be understood as a perpetually if not permanently compromised desire to live, and in this sense, a move beyond or away from Spinoza's claim that the desire to live well emerges at once with the desire to live. Or rather, with Freud, we might say that the desire to live well emerges at once with the desire to live, but also, always, with the desire to die, if not more explicitly with the desire to murder. In this way, we can understand Freud's remark in this context that the categorical imperative is derived from the Oedipus complex. If I am obligated to treat every other human being as an end in himself or herself, it is only because I wish some of them dead and so must militate against that wish in order to maintain an ethical bearing. This is a formulation that is not so far removed from Nietzsche's insistence in *On the Genealogy of Morals* that the categorical imperative is soaked in blood.

Freud's view certainly seems to counter Spinoza's, since for Spinoza, self-preservation seems always to coincide with virtue. Although Spinoza does make room for a deconstitution of the self, or rather an attrition of its desire to live, he would surely dispute the claim that virtue is any part of what *de*constitutes the self; the measure of virtue is precisely the extent to which the self is preserved and the perseverance and enhancement of the *conatus* takes place. And yet, this fairly clear position is already muddled by two other propositions. The first is that the desire to live implicates desire in a matrix of life that may well, at least partially, deconstitute the "I" who endeavors to live. I opened this essay by asking whether it is clear in what Spinozistic self-preservation consists, since perseverance does not seem to be exclusively defined as the preservation of *this* singular self; there may well be a principle of the deconstitution of singularity at work. It may not be possible to say that this deconstitution of singularity parallels the workings of the death drive, but the idea becomes easier to entertain when we consider the second proposition at issue here, that it is possible for a self to acquire an external form, to be animated by an external cause and not be able to form an idea of this alien nature as it works its way with one's own desire. This means that the "I" is already responsive to alterity in ways that it cannot always control, that it absorbs external forms, even contracts them, as one might contract a disease. This means that desire, like the Freudian conception of the drive, is a border concept, always assembled from the workings of this body here in relation to an ideation that is impressed upon it from elsewhere. Those alien forms that the "I" assumes come from the matrix of life, and they constitute, in part, the specters of lives that are gone as well as modes of animating an other, assuming that externality internally so that a certain incorporation ensues, one that acts psychically in ways for which one has no clear idea. In melancholy, we find ourselves acting as the other would have acted, using her speech, donning his clothes. A certain active mode of substitution occurs, such that the other comes not only to inhabit the "I," but to constitute an external force that acts within—a mode of psychic operation without which no subjectivity can proceed. Who acts when the one who is lost from life is reanimated in and by the one who remains, who is transformed by the loss and whose desire becomes the desire to infuse continuing life into what is gone and puts its own life at risk in the course of that endeavor?

Of course, this is not quite Spinoza's thought, though it is something that, in his language and through his terms, we might well begin to think. As we turn to Spinoza's political philosophy, we find that desire is deconstituted from another direction. We can understand how the desire to live runs the risk of deconstituting the self only once we understand the *common life* that desire desires. This common life, in turn, can perhaps be properly understood only if we make the move from ethics to politics and to a consideration of how singularity thrives in and through what Spinoza refers to as the multitude. I would like to approach this conception of Spinoza's through an examination of Levinas's critique of him. In short, Levinas takes Spinoza to represent the principle of self-preservation and interprets this as a kind of self-preoccupation and, indeed, a closing off to the ethical demands that come from the Other. In this sense, Levinas claims that Spinoza can only offer a notion of the social world in which the individual is primary, and in which ethical obligations fail to be acknowledged.

In an interview with Richard Kearney, Levinas makes clear that his own view of ethics must depart from Spinoza's. For Levinas, the human relation to the other is prior to the ontological relation to one-self.[13] And though Levinas does not ask in what self-preservation consists for Spinoza, he seems to assume that the relation to the Other is foreclosed from that domain.

> The approach to the face is the most basic mode of responsibility. . . . The face is not in front of me (*en face de moi*), but above me; it is the other before death, looking through and exposing death. Secondly, the face is the other who asks me not to let him die alone, as if to do so were to become an accomplice in his death. Thus the face says to me: you shall not kill. In the relation to the face I am exposed as a usurper of the place of the other. The celebrated "right to existence" that Spinoza called the *conatus essendi* and defined as the basic principle of all intelligibility is challenged by the relation to the face. Accordingly, my duty to respond to the other suspends my natural right to self-survival, *le droit vitale*. My ethical relation of love for the other stems from the fact that the self cannot survive by itself alone, cannot find meaning within its own being-in-the-world. . . . To expose myself to the vulnerability of the face is to put my ontological right to existence into question. In ethics, the other's right to exist has primacy over my own, a primacy epitomized in the ethical edict: you shall not kill, you shall not jeopardize the life of the other.[14]

Levinas goes on to say, "there is a Jewish proverb which says that 'the other's material needs are my spiritual needs'; it is this disproportion or asymmetry that characterizes the ethical refusal of the first truth of ontology—the struggle to *be*. Ethics is, therefore, against nature because it forbids the murderousness of my natural will to put my own existence first."[15] It would be interesting to find in Levinas a presumption of a natural will murderous in intent, one that must be militated against for the ethical priority of the Other to become established. Such a structure might belie, then, a compensatory trajectory well worth reading, and it would bring him closer to Freud, though, I think, not closer to Spinoza. For though Spinoza's being in its primary ontological mode seeks self-preservation, it does not do this at the expense of the other, and it would be difficult to find something like the equivalent of primary aggression in his work.

Levinas faults Spinoza for believing that through intellectual intuition one can unite oneself with the infinite, whereas for Levinas, the infinite must remain radically other. But Spinoza does not say in what this ostensible unity consists, and it leads Levinas to ally Spinoza with Hegel, a move that is disputed by Pierre Macheray and others within the Althusserian tradition. In fact, sometimes this subtle alliance with Hegel becomes explicit, when, for instance, Levinas remarks in *Alterity and Transcendence* that for Spinoza, "the revelation of the Infinite is rationality itself . . . [and that] knowledge would thus be [for him] only knowledge of knowledge, consciousness only self-consciousness, thought only thought of thought, or Spirit. Nothing would any longer be other: nothing would limit the thought of thought."[16]

Consider the defense of Spinoza's view of sociality, however, provided by Antonio Negri.[17] It would seem that the subject at issue is neither exclusively singular nor fully synthesized into a totality. The pursuit of one's own being, or, indeed, of life, takes one beyond the particularity of one's own life to the complex relation between life and the expression of power. The move from individuality to collectivity is never complete, but is, rather, a movement that produces an irresolvable tension between singularity and collectivity and shows that they cannot be thought without one another, that they are not polar opposites, and that they are not mutually exclusive. The Levinasian tendency to reduce the *conatus* to a desire to be, which is reducible to self-preservation, attempts to lock Spinoza into a model of individuality that belongs to the contractarian tradition to which he is opposed. The individual neither enters into sociality through contract nor becomes subsumed by a collectivity or a multitude. The multitude does not overcome or absorb singularity; the multitude is not the same as a synthetic unity. To understand whether Levinas is right to claim that there is no Other in or for Spinoza, it may be necessary first to grasp that the very distinction between self and Other is a dynamic and constitutive one, indeed, a bind that one cannot flee, if not a bondage in which ethical struggle takes place. Self-preservation for Spinoza does not make sense outside of the context of this bind.

In proposition XXXVII (37) of the *Ethics*, book IV, Spinoza makes clear his difference from a contractarian account of social life. There he maintains: "The good which everyone who seeks virtue wants for himself, he also desires for other men; and this desire is greater as his knowledge of God is greater" (IVP37, 218). In a note to this scholium, he considers how contract theory presupposes "that there is nothing in the state of nature which, by the agreement of all, is good or evil; for everyone who is in the state of nature considers only his own advantage, and decides what is good and what is evil from his own temperament, and only insofar as he takes account of his own advantage. He is not bound by any law to submit to anyone except himself" (IVP37S2, 220). But true self-preservation, as he makes clear in Proposition LIV (54), provides the basis of virtue, in which self-preservation takes place under the guidance of reason. Likewise, freedom, understood as the exercise of reason, consists in disposing humans to reflect upon life, and not on death: "A free man thinks of nothing less than of death, and his wisdom is a meditation on life, not on death" (IVP67, 235).

Similarly, the person who endeavors to preserve his own being finds that this being is not only or exclusively his own. Indeed, the endeavor to persevere in one's being involves living according to reason, where reason illuminates how one's own being is part of what is a common life. "A man who is guided by reason is more free in a state, where he lives according to a common decision, than in solitude" (IVP73, 238). For Spinoza, this means, as well, that hatred should be overcome by love, which means "that everyone who is led by reason desires for others also the good he wants for himself" (IVP73S, 238). Here again we are asked to consider the *simultaneity* of these desires. Just as in desiring to live well we also desire to live, and the one cannot quite be said to precede the other, so here, what one desires for oneself turns out to be, at the same time, what one desires for others. This is not the same as first determining one's own desire and then projecting that desire or extrapolating the desires of others on the basis of one's own desire. This is a desire that must, of necessity, disrupt and disorient the very notion of what is one's own, the very concept of "ownness" itself.

In *The New Spinoza*, Antonio Negri notes that "the absolute is non-alienation, better, it is, positively, the liberation of all social energies in a general *conatus* of the organization of the freedom of all" and then suggests that the subject itself is "recast [by Spinoza] as the multitude."[18]Negri offers an economical formulation of this conception of the multitude, exposing the irreducible tension between two movements in Spinoza's political philosophy: the one in which society is said to act as if according to one mind, the other in which society, by virtue of its expressive structure and dynamic, becomes irreversibly plural. What this means, on the one hand, is that what we might call the general *conatus* turns out to be differentiated and cannot achieve the totality toward which it aims. But what it means, on the other hand, is that singularity is constantly dispossessed in and by its sociality; singularity not only sets a limit on the totalizing possibilities of the social, but, as a limit, it is a singularity that assumes its specificity precisely in the context where it is taken up by a more general *conatus*, where the very life that it seeks deconstitutes its singularity again and again, though only completely in a state of death.

In this way, we can read the implications of Negri's theory for the rethinking of singularity, even though that is the direction opposite to the one in which he moves. He writes, for instance, "if absoluteness is not confronted with the singularity of real powers, it closes back onto itself."[19] But it would seem equally true to claim that the singularity of real powers is what, in its confrontation with absoluteness, establishes an irreversible openness to the process of generalization itself. No general will is achieved, simply put. It is thwarted and articulated through the limiting power of singularity. One might even say that in this sense, singularity is what produces the radically open horizon, the possibility of the future itself. Moreover, if the body is what secures singularity, is what cannot be synthesized into a collectivity, but establishes its limit and its futurity, then the body, in its desire, is what keeps the future open.

However, for this singularity—conceived as a subject—to be powerful, for it to persevere in its desire and to preserve its own power of perseverance, *it cannot be preoccupied with itself.* For Negri, this becomes clear in the experience of *Pietas*:

> *Pietas* is thus the desire that no subject be excluded from universality, as would be the case if one loved the particular. Moreover, by loving universality and by constituting it as a project of reason across subjects, one becomes powerful. If, by contrast, one loves the particular and acts only out of interest, one is not powerful but rather completely powerless, insofar as one is acted on by external things.[20]

Here he refers to love as "a passage so human that it includes all human beings."

Of course, there is the tendency of Spinoza to resolve the singular desire of the subject into a collective unity, and this comes through when he claims, for instance, that "Man ... can wish for nothing more helpful to the preservation of his being than that all should so agree in all things that the minds and bodies of all would compose, as it were, one mind and one body" (IVP18S, 210). This is a situation, however, for which man *can wish*, but it is this wish, not the fulfillment, that constitutes the ontological condition of humanness. Indeed, Spinoza refers to the possibility of a unity of mind and body through a figure, "as it were," signifying that this unity is only conjectured, but cannot be established on certain ground. Something operates as a resistance to this longed-for unification, and this is linked to his abiding materialism, to the radically nonconceptualizable persistence of the body.[21]

Although Levinas's criticism is not yet met, we can see already that it would be a mistake to read self-preservation as if it were self-preoccupation, as if it were possible without the love that "includes all human beings" or the desire that is at once the desire for oneself and for all others. We might still conclude, however, that the Other is not radically and inconceivably Other for Spinoza, and that would be right. But are the ethical consequences of this nonabsolute difference as serious as Levinas takes them to be? After all, in Spinoza there is nevertheless what resists the collapse of the subject into a collective unity. It seems that "the Other" is not quite the word for what *cannot* be collapsed into this unity. It is desire itself, and the body. For Levinas, this would be an impossibility, since desire is precisely what must be suspended for the ethical relation to the Other to emerge. This is where the divergence from Spinoza seems most definite. For what cannot be collapsed into collective unity, from one perspective, is what cannot be collapsed into a purely individualist conception of the *conatus*, from another. Desire to persevere in one's being implicates one in a common life, but the body returns as an ineradicable condition of singularity, only to bear precisely the desire that undoes the sense of one's body or, indeed, one's self, as purely or enduringly one's own.

Interestingly, Levinas remarks that "the humanity of man ... is a rupture of being," and for Spinoza, in a parallel move, it is desire that has this rupture as part of its own movement, a movement from singularity to collectivity and from collectivity to an irreducible plurality. The disorientation in desire consists of the fact that my own desire is never fully or exclusively my own, but that I am implicated in the sociality, if not the potential universality, of my desire in the very acts by which I seek to preserve and enhance my being. In this sense, the singularizing force of the body and its disorienting trajectory toward the social produce a deconstitution of singularity, one that nevertheless cannot fully be accomplished. At the same time, the production of collectivity is deconstituted by this very singularity that cannot be overridden.

So one might see here that Spinoza provides for a shifting and constant principle of deconstitution, one that operates like the death drive in Freud, but that, in order to remain part of the struggle of life, must not become successful as either suicide or murder. This is a principle of deconstitution that is held in check and that, only in check, can function to keep the future open. There are two points here with which I'd like to conclude, one having to do with Freud, and the other with Levinas.

With regard to Freud, I am not proposing that the body in Spinoza does the covert work of the death drive, but I am suggesting that despite the rather stark differences between the Spinozistic point of view that would identify the desire to live well with the desire to live and the psychoanalytic view in which living well may actually come at a cost to desire itself, there seems to be convergence on the notion that a trajectory in desire works in the service of deconstituting the subject, comporting it beyond itself to a possible dissolution in a more general *conatus*. Significantly, it is in this deconstitution and disorientation that an ethical perspective arises, since it will not suffice to say that I desire to live without at the same time seeking to maintain and preserve the life of the Other.

Spinoza comes to this ethical conclusion in a way that differs from Levinas, but consider that for each, a certain rupture and disorientation of the subject conditions the possibility for ethics. Levinas writes:

The face is what one cannot kill, or at least it is that whose *meaning* consists in saying "thou shalt not kill." Murder, it is true, is a banal fact: one can kill the Other; the ethical exigency is not an ontological necessity. . . . It also appears in the Scriptures, to which the humanity of man is exposed inasmuch as it is engaged in the world. But to speak truly, the appearance in being of these "ethical peculiarities"—the humanity of man—is a rupture of being. It is significant, even if being resumes and recovers itself.[22]

If, as Levinas says, citing scripture, the Other's material needs are my spiritual needs, then I am able, spiritually, to apprehend the Other's material needs and put those needs first. For Spinoza, the distinction between material and spiritual needs would not be a secure one, since spiritual needs will end up, within this life, depending upon the body as their source and continuing condition. But it will turn out, nonetheless, that I cannot secure my needs without securing the Other's. The relation between the "I" and the "you" is not, for Spinoza, asymmetrical, but it will be inherently unstable, since my desire emerges in this twofold way, simultaneously for myself and as some more general *conatus*. In a way, these two positions, allied with Freud's, concerning the death drive held in check, underscore the limits of the narcissistic approach to desire and lay out a possibility for a differentiated collective life that is not based in violence, eluding the double specter of narcissism or, indeed, property, on the one hand, and violence either to another or to oneself, on the other. But recourse neither to property nor to violence as final value is necessitated by any of these positions.

What I have been exploring here, though, is a set of approaches to ethics that honor desire without collapsing into the egomaniacal defense of what is one's own, of ownership, and that honor the death drive without letting it emerge as violence to oneself or to another. These are the makings of an *ethics under pressure*, one that would be constituted as a struggle and one that has "anxiety," rather than conviction as its condition.

Let me mention two trajectories that emerge from this framework, and I'll let them stand as dissonant paths. The first belongs to Primo Levi, whose death is generally regarded as a suicide, although there was no note. He fell or threw himself down the stairs of his apartment and was found dead. The death left open the question of whether this was an accident or a purposeful action. The idea is that either he lost his footing, or he gave up his footing. There was no one else there, so the thesis that he was pushed finds no evidence in reality. But I have always been perplexed by this last inference, only because certainly one can be pushed without someone literally there to push you. And the difference between the push and the fall is a complex one, as he himself tells us, for instance, in one of the vignettes he relays in *Moments of Reprieve*. There, he speaks about a Jew interned at Auschwitz who stumbles and falls regularly. Levi writes that every time it seemed like an accident, but there was something purposeful about the fall, that it enacted some pressure that this man was under, some difficulty staying standing, relying on gravity. And surely we might wonder how it might have been to try to stand and walk in the camps, to rely on gravity and its implicit thesis that there is an earth there to receive you. And surely also, if we think about all the pushing that took place there, why would that push cease at the moment that physical contact is relieved? Why wouldn't that push continue to have a life of its own, pushing on beyond the push, exceeding the physicality of the push to attain a psychic form and an animation with a force of its own?

When Levi speaks of suicide in *The Drowned and the Saved*, he writes, "suicide is born from a feeling of guilt that no punishment has attenuated." And following that, he remarks that imprisonment was experienced as punishment, and then, within parentheses, he adds: "if there is punishment, there must have been guilt."[23] In other words, he offers here an account of a certain guilt that takes hold as a consequence of punishment, a guilt based on an inference that one has done something to deserve the punishment. This guilt is, of course, preferable when the alternative is to grasp the utter contingency and arbitrariness of torture, punishment, and extermination. At least with guilt, one continues to have agency. With the arbitrary infliction of torture, one's agency is annihilated, as well. This "guilt" that receives a knowing account within parentheses nevertheless becomes, within his text, a fact, a given, a framework, so that he asks, mercilessly, whether he did enough in the camps to help others; he remarks that everyone felt guilty about not helping others,[24] and then he asks his reader and himself whether any of us would have the proper moral armature to fight the seductions of fascism. He comes to accept self-accusation as the posture he must assume with respect to his own actions, actions that were not, by the way, collaborationist.

Levi's guilt comes to frame a morality that holds those in the camp accountable for what they did and did not do. In this sense, his morality occludes the fact that agency itself was widely vitiated, that what might count as an "I" was either sequestered or deadened, as Charlotte Delbo makes clear. It defends against that offense, the offense against a recognition that the ego, too, was decimated. But more importantly, it enters into the cycle by which the guilt produced by punishment requires further punishment for its own relief. If, as he claims, "suicide is born from a feeling of guilt that no punishment has attenuated," we might add that no punishment *can* attenuate such guilt, since the guilt is groundless and endless and the punishment that would alleviate it is responsible for its infinite reduplication. It is over and against this particularly bad infinity, then, that suicide most probably emerges for someone like Levi. But what this means is that we cannot answer the question of whether he fell by accident, threw himself, or was pushed, since the scene of agency had become, doubtless, fractured into those simultaneous and co-constituting actions. He fell by accident, surely, if what we mean by that is that his fall was not the result of his own agency; he was pushed, surely, by an agency of punishment that continued to work upon him; he threw himself, surely, for he had, through his morality, become the executor of his self-torture, believing as he did that he was not and could not be punished enough.

The second and last remark concerning an ethics under pressure, then: we see this ethical difficulty alive in antiwar practices in Israel by those who oppose the occupation of Palestinian lands or call for a new polity that would leave Zionism behind; the collective efforts to rebuild demolished Palestinian homes; the efforts of Ta-ayush, a Jewish-Arab coalition to bring food and medicine to those suffering within the Occupied Territories; and the institutional practices of villages like Neve Shalom to foster Jewish-Arab self-government and joint ownership and to create communities and schools in which my desire is not powerful or self-preserving unless it permits for a disorientation by yours, in your power of self-preservation and perseverance. I'll cite to you from an e-mail from a friend of mine in Israel, since I think we can see that it is possible to base an ethics on one's own situation, one's own desire, without the relation to the other becoming pure projection or an extension of one's self. Her name is Niza Yanay, and she is a sociologist at Ben Gurion University who worries that the Supreme Court has lost its power in Israel, that military rule is ascending, that proposals to relocate Palestinians are being actively debated in the Knesset. She writes,

> In the elections a few months ago a friend and I both voted for the communist party which was a Jewish-Palestinian party but now is mostly an Arab-Palestinian party with almost no Jewish supporters. We felt that it is utterly important to strengthen the power of the Arabs in the parliament, and to show solidarity with them. Sami Shalom Shitrit, a poet and a writer, said in a small gathering before the election that if in 1933 he had been a German and Christian he would have looked very carefully to find a Jewish party to vote for. I was very moved by it, but it also gave me the shivers because we are not that far from 1933.

We are not in 1933, but we are not that far, and it is in that proximate difference that a new ethics must be thought. When discussions of "transfers" of populations have begun in the Knesset and vengeance seems to be the principle invoked on both sides of the conflict, it is crucial to find and value the "face" that will put an end to violence. To be responsive to that face, however, demands a certain self-dispossession, a move away from self-preservation as the basis or, indeed, the aim of ethics.

Whereas some locate the belief that self-preservation is the basis of ethics with Spinoza, and others suggest that Spinoza forecloses the forms of negativity that Freud so aptly describes under the rubric of the death drive, I have been trying to suggest that Spinoza's view leads neither to the defense of a simple individualism nor to the forms of territoriality and rights of self-defense usually associated with doctrines of self-persistence. Within the Jewish frameworks for ethics that presume the superego and its cruelties as a precondition of ethical bearing or that claim that forms of political sociality are based on the unity of a people, conceived spatially, Spinoza enters with a form of political solidarity that moves beyond both suicide and the kinds of political unities associated with territoriality and nationalism. That he is doubtless still part of an intra-Jewish quarrel on the meaning and domain of ethics seems true, but that he is also outside the tradition, indeed, providing models for working with and alongside that "outside," seems equally true.

But what is perhaps most important is to see that there are the contours of an ethic here in which the death drive is held in check, one that conceives a community in its irreducible plurality and would oppose every nationalism that seeks to eradicate that condition of a nontotalizable sociality. It would be an ethic that not only avows the desire to live, but recognizes that desiring life means desiring life for you, a desire that entails producing the political conditions for life that will allow for regenerated alliances that have no final form, in which the body, and bodies, in their precariousness and their promise, indeed, even in what might be called their ethics, incite one another to live.

To Sense What Is Living in the Other

Hegel's Early Love

There are not many manifest reasons to think about Hegel and love together. First of all, Hegel is hardly lovable to most people; many readers do not want to take the time to sort out those sentences. Second, the language of love is usually understood to be a direct proclamation or a lyrical expression of some kind. Third, love has a relation to images and motions, to what we imagine time and again or, rather, to a form of imagining and moving that seems to take us up into its repetitions and elaborations. So the topic of love seems an odd way to approach Hegel, whose language is dense, who explicitly devalues nonlinguistic forms of art, and for whom direct address and lyrical style seem equally remote. And yet it was a topic to which he turned in his early work, where "love" is the name for what animates and what deadens, and his views have clear implications for thinking about the senses and aesthetics more generally. In the years prior to writing *The Phenomenology of Spirit* (1807), for example, Hegel wrote a short essay called "Love" (1797–98), a fragment of which remains.[1] And we find further remarks in a small piece now called "Fragment of a System" (1800).[2] Later, it seems, love falls away, or is pushed away, or becomes silently absorbed into his writing on spirit.

How do we read Hegel reading love? Is there love in his language? His early writing pushes forward with declarative sentences. This is not simply because he knows the truth and declares it with great confidence, but because the declarative sentence is a way of pushing forward and pushing off. One sentence lays the groundwork for the next, and an idea is probed or developed without precisely being derived in a sequential way. In fact, although we could try, as readers of Hegel surely have, to extract the propositions from his writings, organize them into arguments that rely on primary and secondary premises and logically derived conclusions, I want to suggest that something else is happening here. When a sentence is declared or arrives in the form of a declaration, something is being shown, a particular way of looking at the world is instated, a certain way of taking a stance is enacted. We might say that a point of view is enacted in the sentence form. So when the next sentence follows, it is not always an amplification of that same point of view. Sometimes it is another point of view that critically comments on the first or shows us an unexpected consequence of the first. Sometimes that can happen over the course of a few sentences, or even a paragraph or two, and we remain pondering within the terms of that framework being enacted for that time. But then a certain turn takes place—sometimes it is within a subordinate clause, or sometimes it takes place through a shift in tone or modulation of voice. At such a point, we see that the original point of view that was confidently declared within a single or short series of propositions has slowly been called into question. For that particular claim to be called into question is not quite the same as exposing a basic corrosion within the propositional or the declarative sequence, and yet something of the confidence of the initial sequence is rattled by what comes next. And what has come next actually seems to follow from what came before, which means that the seeds of unrest—what Hegel time and again called

Unruhe—were there from the start; they were simply unseen or set aside at the beginning of the exposition. So this unsettling happens, but neither as the sudden outbreak of nihilism nor as the violent renunciation of what came before. In the midst of the development of the exposition, the declarative form has lost its confidence. This can happen simply by a repetition of the declarative form in a similarly confident mode, at which point the reader is confronted by two competing claims articulated with equal confidence. At such junctures, we might ask, does the authorial voice retain control over its material? Or is there something about the material itself, its very elaboration, that involves a reversal? The voice has reversed itself without exactly vilifying itself and without exactly repudiating what has come before. What, we might ask, do such convolutions have to do with love?

Hegel enacts a reversal in his exposition of love that belongs as much to the topic as to its exposition. We might say that now we understand that something in the nature of love is reversible or reverses itself, and we have to find a mode of writing that acknowledges or explains that reversibility. The mode of presentation has to conform to the demands of what is presented; what "is" requires its presentation in order to be at all. In other words, the presentation of love is a development or temporal elaboration of the object of love, so we cannot rightly distinguish love itself as an object, theme, or problem from its presentation (which does not mean that the object is reducible to how it is presented, only that the object becomes available only through that presentation). Love cannot remain a mute and internal feeling, but requires the presentation of love in some way. I do not mean that all love must be confessed or declared to qualify as love, but only that the declarative mode is not simply an idiosyncratic way of approaching the problem of love for the Hegel of 1797. Love has to develop in time; it has to take on a certain shape or form that cannot be restricted to a single proposition. There has to be something like a chain of sentences, declarative and interrogative, that not only records a growing confidence and its undoing, but initiates unexpected modes of arrival, all as ways of enacting those movements as part of the phenomenon itself. After all, the phenomenon of love, no matter how mute or vociferous, no matter how inward or outward, has something of its own logic—one that unfolds or develops in time and that, as we will see, never actually blossoms into final form, but remains defined by its indefinite openness.

One perhaps expects a totalizing system from Hegel, but that error has outlived its time. In the *Phenomenology*, he establishes this openness in his analysis of how indexicals work.[3] In relation to the "now," that most immediate moment, it turned out that the "now" was always past by the time we referred to it. We lost the "now"—or saw it vanish—at the moment of pointing to it, which means that acts of reference do not precisely capture their referent. Indeed, the temporal problem that emerges when anyone tries to point to the "now" establishes a belatedness that affects all referentiality. The problem was not that pointing to the "now" pushed it back into the "then," but that the act of pointing, the act of indicating, was always belated and that only when the "now" becomes "then" can it become reflected on as a "now." A temporal lag separates the language that seeks to indicate the "now" from the moment indicated, and so there is a difference between the time of the indication and the time of what is indicated. In this way, language always misses its mark, and has to, in order to refer to that time at all. In this sense, the "now" is invariably "then" by the time it becomes available to us in language (which is, by the way, the only way it becomes available, since there is no unmediated relation to the "now"). Hegel is no vitalist; neither does he believe that the immediate is available to us without mediation, even though time and again he will consider those experiences that seem to us to be most immediate, most clearly without mediation. "Mediation" has at least two different meanings here: first, whatever becomes available to us within experience has been rendered external and has been reflected back to us by some external medium; second, whatever becomes available to us, in passing through or being reflected back to us by what is external, is always at a distance from its original location and its original time. In other words, a certain displacement in time and space constitutes the condition of knowing, what Hegel often refers to as a "return" of the object. The object must leave, become something other, over and against me, and it must also return, become something indissociable from me, however foreign. How it returns is invariably different from how it leaves, so it never quite returns to the same place, which means that its "return" is something of a misnomer.

As we think about the "now," there is always some operation of time that exceeds what we call the "now" and without which we would not be able to name the "now" at all. The same is true of whatever we might call the "end" of a process—indeed, by the time we name the end, it is already over, which means that the time of naming passes beyond that end into another register of time; the end, if nameable, if indicated, turns out to be not quite so final. What name we give to this time that exceeds the end is unclear. Perhaps if there is a linguistic way to indicate this time, it will be one that operates within a sense of the belated. And if we think that this is a problem of mournfulness, a kind of mournfulness implied by the indicative, we may be right. How might we return to love from this understanding? Is there some persistence of time that opens up at the end, or beyond the end, or even a strange poetic function of the end? How do love and loss enter the formulation? Is there some way to avert mournfulness implied by Hegel's view, or does mourning turn out to precede love itself?

Hegel's fragment on love begins with the question, how do those who participate in religion negotiate between their individuality and belonging to a community? Interestingly, from the start, one cannot ask about whether the individual is separated from the community or whether the individual is in some ways unified with the community without understanding the relation of the individual to property, or to what Hegel calls the "object" or "object world."[4] If religion involves either the collective ownership of objects or their sacrifice, then individuals give up all rights of possession to them. Under conditions in which an individual's value is derived from his possession, he loses his value for himself when he vacates all forms of possessive individualism; indeed, in Hegel's words, when the individual loses all of what he possesses, he comes to despise himself—or so it would appear under conditions in which objects give the person his value and where objects are possessed as property.

Self-hatred has entered the picture rather suddenly here, as have the requirements of communal existence. Religion is first formulated as a form of community membership that requires the negation or sacrifice of individual property and, as a corollary, the individual's negation of himself—one that takes the affective form of self-hatred. How, we might ask, will self-hatred find its way into love? And within this economy, does self-love follow only from the possession of property?

The second problem that Hegel engages is somewhat surprising, since it would seem that he is inquiring into the conditions for a living relationship between the individual and his world. For the moment, the community and community membership are set aside, and a new point of departure is introduced. There is a second implication of the individual's separation from his object world. The first was self-hatred, since the individual seeks to give up possession of himself, but is not fully successful. The second implication is equally alarming: the object itself has become dead. Alas, one hates oneself, and the object world is dead under conditions in which property confers value. And yet Hegel seeks to counter these conclusions by asking after the possibility of a living union of individuals and objects: Is this an alternative conception of religion, and is it one that requires love or is in some sense composed of love? When he writes, "The object is dead," we are compelled to ask, how did the object die?[5] Is this the general form of the object and, in that sense, all objects? Is it dead for all time?

There are two forms by which objects die: sacrifice and property. At first it seems that Hegel cautions us against giving up property, if that means giving up all material things, all materiality. And then it seems he is trying to find a way to affirm matter and the object world without letting them be reduced to property. The text first asks us to imagine and enter into that configuration of the world in which an individual, one who has not fully given up his individuality, is confronted by a world of dead objects, surrounded by that world that has been established through the actions by which all personal property is sacrificed for the communal good. Under these conditions, in which individuals are deprived of all property, they are also deprived of a living relation to objects—objects become dead. And what affective life becomes possible for individuals under such conditions? They come to love what is dead. They remain living and loving in relation to an object, or set of objects, or indeed an object world, that is dead, and in this sense they remain in a vital relation to what is dead. Indeed, dead objects constitute the other term in a love relationship. And so under these conditions, love loves a matter that is indifferent to the one who loves. This relationship is precisely not a living union. When Hegel begins, then, to make remarks about "love's essence at this level" (in seiner innersten Natur),[6] he is not telling us about love's essence for all time, but only how the essence of love is constituted under conditions of compelled sacrifice, that is, where religion requires individuals to separate from their objects as a stipulation of community membership.[7]

Hegel is now trying to occupy the point of view of one who has complied with the obligation to lose the object world, to live in a world of dead objects, and to live out the consequences of this particular mode of love in which one loves only objects that are dead. It is, of course, interesting that love itself is not nullified under these conditions. Rather, love takes on a new form; one might even say, love takes on a specifically historical form. The one who lives within such a configuration has not only lost the object world, but continues to love what has become dead to him; at the same time, he remains confident that his loss will be compensated, that some eternity or infinity will be gained, and then he will be free of all matter. And yet, if within such a scheme matter must be refused or lost, if matter must become dead matter, then even the individual's own bodily matter will become dead for him. In other words, if the individual loses and continues to love that matter that has become dead for him, and he himself has become dead matter, then the individual now loses and loves his lost materiality. Dead to himself, he lives on—melancholically. He loses what he can never fully lose. And what is dead to him is also the condition of his living.

Under such circumstances, what reason can the individual give for his own material existence? The problem is not only that he is surrounded by dead objects, but that as a body that must be separated from a pure spirit, he has become a dead object for himself. And within this experience, an experience conditioned by a set of very specific religious stipulations, a reversal takes place: "the individual cannot bear to think of himself as this nullity" (*nur das dürre Nichts*).[8] Again, Hegel has entered into, has started to enact, the reversal and paradox that will turn out to define the sacrifice of personal property for the religious community; it now turns out that the individual who complies with these stipulations, or rather lives within the world structured by these stipulations, is precisely unable to bear loving dead objects and becoming for himself a lost and dead object to which he remains ineluctably attached. The individual does not quite reach infinity, but now articulates a new region of the unbearable ("in diesem sich zu denken kann freilich der Mensch nicht ertragen").[9] Hegel implies here that there are limits to what is bearable; we are being asked to consider the requirements that establish what will be bearable within human love. The individual who thinks of himself as a dead object is not bearable to himself, but why? First, because there is a consciousness of what is unbearable—unbearability is the form that this consciousness takes, and insofar as it takes place, emerges, it shows or enacts that some form of consciousness has already or has still transcended the dead matter that the existing individual is supposed to be. But the problem is not only epistemological or even logical. Rather, the individual suffers a deformation of love in which he now loves himself as a dead thing. If all matter must become dead (sacrificed, devalued), and he is himself a material being, he must become dead. To accomplish this task within life, however, he himself must be alive, which means that he must remain alive, dedicated to the unbearable fate of becoming dead while alive. His fate becomes anguish.

It may seem odd that Hegel then proffers the remark "nothing carries the root of its own being in itself" (keines trägt die Wurzel seines Wesens in sich), underscoring that all determinate existence comes from somewhere or something that is not itself.[10] Within such a configuration, or under those particular requirements of religion, it turned out that the individual could have only contempt for his determinate specificity, his own status as a material being, and for the material dimension of the object world. They were excluded from the spiritual and so became a dead part of life, absolutely differentiated from the spiritual and so absolutely dead. And in this way, they assumed an absolute status as nonliving and nonspiritual. Such a view, however, failed to give an account within religious terms of why and how material objects come into being. Hence, Hegel shows not only that the original formulation he offered of religion is partial and impossible—it unwittingly makes dead matter absolute, it makes the individual dead to himself or plunges him into the practice of self-hatred that could be escaped only through his own nullification as a living being, a condition that proves to be unbearable—but also that it fails to understand the religious significance of why and how the material world comes into being. Material existence arrives from elsewhere. In this sense, at least for now, this is what is meant by "nothing carries the root of its own being in itself."

Another set of declarations follows, and it would seem that now Hegel is showing his cards. He starts to say what true love actually is, and at least in this version (and we have to be mindful that it is a version, that something might happen to this version to unsettle the declarative confidence of its presentation), that true love is a living union and that it seems to happen between persons who are alike in power (and so a principle of equality is entered into the formulation) and where neither is dead to the other. Love involves not being dead for the other, and the other not being dead for one. The scene is dyadic, and thus we might well wonder what happened to the community. Did community collapse into coupledom? And what happened to the object world? Are objects still there, in nascent form, or have we suddenly entered into a couple form shorn of both community and property? This love, we are told, is neither understanding nor reason, but is rather a feeling ("Sie ist ein Gefühl"). Or at least he defines it at first as a single feeling, before promptly beginning a set of revisions. We are, as readers, to start from the claim that love is a feeling, only to learn rather rapidly, within the very next phrase, that it is "yet not a single feeling" (aber nicht ein einzelnes Gefühl).[11] OK, it is a feeling and yet not a single feeling, but with the second claim, Hegel is not exactly negating the first; he is accumulating propositions; the one trips over the next, and something of a chain begins to take shape. Although love is always singular, it cannot be restricted to the singular instance or its presentation or declaration. It takes a singular form, and yet must always also take more than a singular form. If we ask, what is that more than singular form that love takes? we are told that a singular feeling is "only a part and not the whole of life" (es nur ein Teilleben, nicht das ganze Leben ist).[12] So here we return to the problem of life, or rather to what is living, its synecdochal animation, and we recur to the notion that love must be living if it is to be actual and true love. And yet this living feeling, the one that is singular and nonsingular, connects to a greater sense of what is living or to a set of living processes that exceed the single feeling of aliveness that any of us might have. This connection is not exactly identity and not exactly not.

We have been following the presentation from the point of view of the individual subject and its singular and living feeling of love—one that excludes all oppositions and so seems to be all-embracing. We then leave the perspective of the living to take the point of view, as it were, of life itself. Now we are to understand something more about that life than the singular feeling of life in love. The singular feeling of life suddenly gives rise to "Life" as the subject of the sentence that follows, and we are told what Life does through a personification that animates or gives life to the concept of life itself. Life is said to "drive on"; it "disperses itself" in a manifold of feelings "with a view to finding itself in the entirety of this manifold" (drängt sich das Leben durch Auflösung zur Zerstreuung in der Mannigfaltigkeit der Gefühle und um sich in diesem Ganzen der Mannigfaltigkeit zu finden).[13] So life is personified here, given agency, not simply as a rhetorical device that somehow falsifies or embellishes what it really is. The reversal as well as the displaced agency is meant to show that the development of the phenomenon of love involves a displacement of that purely subjective point of view—some dispossession of the self takes place in love. Internal to the singular and living feeling of love is an operation of life that exceeds and disorients the perspective of the individual. That operation of life has to be followed as a process or development that is instantiated in the absolute singularity of the perspective that it also exceeds.

The couple form does not survive this insight very well. That feeling of life, that is, the process of life that pervades all feeling, and not just the singular one, will determine and exceed its instances. Indeed, even though we are starting to understand that love must be living to be love, it will turn out that life itself can never be contained or exhausted by love. Life takes on a certain form in love, what Hegel calls a "duplicate."[14] It is embodied by a figure, the human form of the one whom one loves. But it would be an error to say that the one whom one loves is life itself. Of course, we do sometimes make mad proclamations of this kind. But even so, it is but one of the erroneous rhetorical forms that belong to love, an error, an overanimation, that bespeaks some truth and some untruth. The other is not life itself, because the other is a bounded being, determinate and material and so having come into living existence, bound to pass out of it, as well; whatever union is achieved in love is not an absolute overcoming of difference, the finitude by which two individuals are separated, but also the finitude that implies mortality. The couple does not dissolve into life itself without dying, since each would have to relinquish its determinate living form. And yet as separate and persisting forms, each is understood "to sense what is living in the other."[15] This is an important formulation, since for Hegel, there is something living in love, and has to be, even though love can never be the whole of life.

What we have been calling the determinateness of the human form, its bodily matter, establishes the one who loves as a living being who senses what is living in the other.[16] Sense or sensing thus emerges precisely on the condition of separateness; the one is not the life of the other, and the other is not the life of the one. And yet this sensing of the life of the other is possible only on the condition that both are living beings. It will be interesting to know whether that sensing of the life of the other is possible only on the condition of equality, something that Hegel introduced at the beginning of the lecture. Is inequality a mode of deadness? If the other is unequal, is the other also in some sense dead, or only partially alive? Is treating the other as unequal a way of deadening that other or becoming dead to the other and / or oneself?

So when Hegel makes a claim such as "In the lovers there is no matter" (An Liebenden ist keine Materie), does he accept that as true?[17] What purpose does this declaration serve in the presentation he is offering? Has he not already told us that it won't work for lovers to overcome their matter? If their "living union" implies that they must come together without matter, then their love is not a bodily love. Can there be, then, no living matter in Hegel, or, at least, no living matter at this moment of love? The text seems to open this very question, seems, in fact, to circle around this question as its most fundamental and reiterated longing. Is he at this moment simply telling us that disembodied love is yet another erroneous way of configuring love? As his discussion continues, he makes clear that lovers seek to overcome this problem of matter in their quest to be immortal. And sure enough, this matter persists—indeed, I would suggest that a certain obstinate materialism runs throughout Hegel—and the lovers are unable fully to negate the difference between them. We might say that their bodies get in the way of their union, and there is no way of getting around this fact except, we might conjecture, through some sort of murder or suicide (or a social practice for which murder or suicide has been made into the structuring principle). Interestingly, Hegel does not say that one consciousness becomes indignant when it learns that it cannot fully negate the difference, the dead matter, that is the other. In his language, love itself is described as indignant. So this is an indignation that belongs properly to love, an indignation without which love itself cannot be thought. As readers, we are asked to shift perspectives here, even to give up on our own identifications; a displacement or decentering happens, but not one that simply leaves us there, confused and defeated. We are going somewhere, and this reversal is part of that passage, but to where precisely? The reversal is our reversal, to be sure, but it is also one that belongs to love, so even though we have lost our orientation, we are now onto something about love itself. My reversal and the one that characterizes love are not parallel experiences or analogies. They are not simply like one another. They are two dimensions of the same phenomenon, and so the text solicits us to think them together, to gather them as they accumulate, in the midst of our not yet knowing. There is no one perspective by which the phenomenon of love can be described. If it can be described, it is only through the shift of perspective and through some way of grasping or gathering those various shifts. They imply one another, and it is only by undergoing these shifts and displacements that we can hope to enact and thus to know love itself.

But let us return to indignation, since it seems to indicate that the union toward which love strives is incomplete, and necessarily so. Hegel refers to that "separable element" (das Trennbare) on which love stumbles, or "a still subsisting independence" (noch vorhandenen Selbständigkeit).[18] There is some "part of the individual that is held back as a

private property" or even "severed" ("jene fühlt sich durch diese ge-
hindert—die Liebe ist unwillig über das noch Getrennte, über ein Ei-
gentum").[19] It would seem that in the face of this obdurate separateness
there is a "raging of love" (Zürnen der Liebe)—Hegel's term. And
linked to this raging is a form of shame ("seine Scham wird zum
Zorn").[20] On the one hand, the individuality of the other precludes
the union, and yet to rage against that individuality is to strike at the
other whom one loves. It is apparently the consciousness of raging or
striking against the other that turns to shame, because, according to
Hegel, "the hostility in a loveless assault does injury to the loving heart
itself" (bei einem Angriff ohne Liebe wird ein liebevolles Gemüt durch
diese Feindseligkeit selbst beleidigt).[21] The formulation leaves unclear
whether the injury is done to the loving heart of the one who rages
and strikes, or if it is the one raged against and struck who is injured.
Perhaps the ambiguous reference implies that it is necessarily both,
since at that moment, the loving heart ceases to be loving; it becomes
a deadening force, even the guardian of what is dead, namely, private
property and the right to that property. So the one who is loved becomes the one to whom one has a right of private property, which means
that the living other has become dead, since, as we know, property
was already described as a form of deadness.

In the midst of this reflection on love, Hegel oddly remarks that
shame is "most characteristic of tyrants, or of girls" ("so müßte man
von den Tyrannen sagen, sie haben am meisten Scham, so wie von Mäd-
chen"), and it makes sense to pause for a moment here.[22] Why does
shame enter here? Shame is clearly a difficult and uneasy way of being
"reflected back" to oneself. One sees oneself through the eyes of the
other, and so shame is a form of being linked to the visual perspective of the other. But who is experiencing shame in the scenes that
Hegel describes? And is shame itself a form of love, or one of its de-
formations? Is it the girls he has in mind who are said to feel shame
when they yield their bodies for money—prostitutes, or those whose
work is sex? Are these women included in that group he conjectures

as "vain women" (den eitlen)?²³ Are they the same as or different from those women who have as their sole aim the desire to fascinate, which seems, in Hegel's view, to be something distinct from loving or being loved? Tyrants are not much described here, but they are gathered together with sex workers, seemingly part of an increasing crowd of loveless figures, and we have to ask why. Is it that the women are tyrannical because they sell their bodies or use them for the purposes of fascination? Or are the women figured as subject to a tyrannical force? A tyrant imposes his will absolutely, treats others as subordinates, chattel, or private property. Are they mentioned here because Hegel is pointing to a tyrannical possibility within love itself, the risk of tyrannizing or being tyrannized? It would be odd to think of those fascinating girls as exercising a tyrannical force, unless someone felt tyrannized by their fascinating forces, or indeed to think of both tyrants and sex workers as equally prone to a similar shame. Yet it seems that for Hegel, shame is what is associated with such institutions in which bodies are instrumentalized for the will of another, perhaps as well that when love takes on the form of inequality and subordination, shame follows—even if it is only Hegel's shame at the thought. This seems to apply equally to the use of the sexual body for the purposes of making money and the use of others' bodies as personal property or slave labor. The shame seems to be part of the practice, but it also seems to follow from an aggressive, subordinating, and / or instrumentalizing dimension of love itself.

Hegel seems aware, in a fashion nearly Kleinian, that love has within it a hostile element. Shame seems to emerge precisely as a result of being conscious of the hostility in love that keeps love from ever being absolute. But the way he puts it suggests that the body itself keeps that union from being complete: "shame enters only through the recollection of the body, through the presence of an [exclusive] personality or the sensing of an [exclusive] individuality" (Die Scham tritt nur ein durch die Erinnerung an den Körper, durch persönliche Gegenwart, beim Gefühl der Individualität).²⁴ The body stands in the way of union. It is separate; it is mortal; it can be encountered as a fixed barrier. But what is the experience through which that obdurate separateness is overcome? That happens only through an exchange in which giving is enhancing and receiving is a form of giving. Hegel refers to forms of touch and contact in which consciousness of separateness is overcome. This is not a merging into oneness, but a certain suspension of separateness. Predictably, this brief excursus on sexuality produces a child as its result, so the two bodies achieve unity only in what proves to be separate from them, their offspring, something of them and beyond them both. The couple now dissolves through a triangulation that it is compelled to produce.

But the child is not the ultimate problem. Lovers never quite get over what is dead between them. They are in connection with much that is dead, he writes. There seems to be always a question of property, of what they each own, and also whether something in the other is owned or capable of being owned by another. Wherever there are rights to property, so, too, is there some deadness. Some ambiguity persists here: not only do the objects that they own, objects that are external to both of them, become a form of deadness between them, but there is "a dead object in the power of one of the lovers" ("Das unter der Gewalt des Einen befindliche Tote ist beiden entgegengesetzt") that stands over and against them, opposing them both.[25] Does the one lover own something that the other does not own? Does the ownership of an external object produce something dead inside the owner, a dead object that somehow resides in or under the power of the owner? And is it something other than its own body? If one has property rights in one's own body, does that not produce deadness in one's love? Even if an object is external and shared, or even if the object is the body itself, regarded as common property, the problem of that deadness is not quite overcome. Hegel gestures near the end of the essay toward the possibility of common property, but does the common overcome the individual, or does it simply make rights of ownership undecidable? He seems to be suggesting that ownership cannot be rightly reconciled with love. For love, you will remember, is love between equals, and property is always a matter of possession and seems to depend on the primacy of the individual: "everything that men possess has the legal form of property" (weil alles, in dessen Besitz die Menschen sind, die Rechtsform des Eigentums hat).[26] To divide property is to divide what is already dead, which means that love, understood as a living and equal exchange, is put out of play. Hegel's fragment ends with no resolution. A question nevertheless emerges from its vacillations: is love reconcilable with marriage, property, even children? And do each of these introduce and sustain some deadness?

In a way, the task for Hegel in this essay and in "Fragment of a System" (1800) is to figure out what keeps alive what is living in love. He strives to understand infinite life, or rather what is infinite in life, and this means discerning a relation that is neither conceptual nor spectatorial. Oddly, "God" becomes the name of all those relations that Hegel will call living relations ("die Beziehungen ohne das Tote").[27] As such, God cannot be reduced to a set of laws, since laws are conceptual and thus, in his terms, dead. So when he imagines a form of aliveness that keeps living, he understands its ideal form as one that, unlike the human lover, carries in itself nothing dead.

Not all laws are bad or wrong, and Hegel was no anarchist. And yet he searches time and again for an "animating law" (belebendes Gesetz) that operates in unity with a manifold that is "then itself animated" (als dann ein belebtes).[28] We move from a consideration of what is living to what is animated, and rather than staying within the simple opposition of law (lifeless) and love (living), we are led to understand a living law, or animated law, and prompted as well to think about how animation works both as a rhetorical feature of this text and as part of its very definition of spirit. As expected, it turns out that death cannot be radically excluded from life or from spirit. We do not overcome the dead, or what is dead, and we cannot bring all that is dead back to life, and yet this notion of a perpetual, if not infinite, aliveness remains alive within his text. Is it a phantasm, a structuring impossibility, a vanishing point of idealization? If reflecting on life is a way of killing off life to some degree, making life provisionally dead or fixed ("fixiertes"), there is no way around this, since we cannot not reflect on life, if we are philosophers in any sense of the term. Conceptually, we cannot understand the living without understanding something of what is dead, since the contrast first makes that determination possible. Life is broken into parts and segments, which means that the apprehension of life is to some extent bound by perspective and a principle of selection. As a result, one part of life has its aliveness at the expense of another, so there is always, from any given perspective within life, some part that is dead to it—siphoned off, foreclosed. And since the living one who occupies any given perspective has had to deaden some part of the field of the living, some part of life can—even must—be dead to another part and alive to another; it all depends on which perspective is enlivened and engaged. Infinite life cannot become an "object" for thought without becoming finite and thus losing its very character. The true infinite is outside of reason, or so Hegel seems to say. And if love is infinite life, then philosophy is forced to withdraw from love in order to continue engaging in reflection and to fulfill the task of crystallizing life. Whatever crystallization philosophy provides invariably gives a finite and spatial form to the infinite—and in some ways stops its time, entering a deadening element into that process. The true infinite is not a product of reflection, and reflection tends to stop time, to establish a set of definite and finite moments. As a result, a philosopher must cease to be a philosopher if he or she wishes to affirm that infinite life named by "love." One could conclude that for Hegel, philosophers are bad lovers. But his point is rather more precise: one name for the deadening element in love is "philosophy."

Or, perhaps, philosophy is just the messenger who brings us the invariably bad news about love. There seems to be no easy way for a living being not to become an object of one sort or another, a site or condition of reflection. The one who loves is a very specific and existing being who cannot overcome his or her finitude through love. And what is worse is that the one who loves also clings to that finitude in a stubborn and insistent way, a furtive form of self-attachment, understood more generally as a refusal to yield. When Hegel ruminates on why religion can somehow elevate life to its infinity, whereas philosophy cannot, he returns again to that recalcitrant part of the self— stubborn, finite, even dead—that refuses to give way. But this time it is a problem not of yielding to another, but of giving up property in oneself. Indeed, although Hegel seems to be in some ways praising the capacities of religion and lamenting the restrictions imposed by philosophy, his exposition surely takes a critical tone when he argues the following: humans destroy some part of themselves on the altar— they become a form of sacrifice, they destroy what belongs to them by establishing all that they own as common property, and they negate any and all objects because of their finiteness, engaging in excesses of asceticism and self-denial. This, Hegel comes to call an "aimless destruction for destruction's sake" ("dies zwecklose Vernichten um des Vernichtens willen"), which proves to be the ultimate religious relation to objects.[29]

But toward the end of this small piece, his tone shifts, as if he has found an alternative. Interestingly enough, it relates to dance. Worship, he tells us, is neither intuitive nor conceptual, but rather "a joyful subjectivity of living beings, of song, or of motions of the body . . . expressions like a solemn oration can become objective and beautiful by rules, namely, dance" ("das Wesen des Gottesdienstes ist . . . vielmehr mit Subjektivität Lebendiger in Freude zu verschmelzen, [vermittels] des Gesanges, der körperlichen Bewegungen, einer Art von subjektiver Äußerung, die, wie die tönende Rede, durch Regel objektiv und schön, zum Tanz werden kann").[30] Dance seems to give concrete meaning to the idea of an animated and animating law. Indeed, dance seems to be singled out grammatically, evincing that moment when bodies come alive in a rule-bound way, but without precisely conforming to any law. When Hegel imagines "happy people" ("glücklichen"), they have clearly minimized without relinquishing their separateness.[31]

He is trying to imagine some operation of love that goes beyond the dyad and property. We move again toward that vanishing point of idealization. Through the invocation of the aesthetic domain, this time one that centers on social motions, Hegel starts to imagine those who neither seek to possess others as their property nor hold on to their personhood as property. The problem is whether the human body or any of the objects with which it engages can be thought or lived outside the property form. For property is what deadens, in his view, which means that love cannot survive anyone holding onto oneself or another as property—both self-preservation (understood as obstinacy) and possession have to become less important than an affirmation of what is living in love. What Hegel failed to realize adequately in this early work is that property is itself animated and animating under conditions of capitalist property relations and that this is the meaning and effect of the fetishism of commodities. They are personified and invested, agential and haunting. Yet Hegel is already in the thrall of personification, writing about what Life does, for instance, as if Life were a person, showing how abstractions sometimes require the sacrifice of what is material and finite, but also underscoring the power of property to rob persons of what is most living in them, including or especially the owners.

What Hegel is articulating in those few decades before Marx's analysis of the commodity is the wish to separate what is animated and animating from the world of property. He does not oppose the world of objects, but wants only to keep that world animated—forever. When objects become property, and property law comes to prevail, the effect is to break down those relations among humans and objects that we might call loving. And this seems to be a different modality from any religious effort to lift the finite into the infinite and have it vanquished there. What Hegel seeks through the idea of animating law (or enlivening form) is something close to a dance, the dance of lovers (not presumptively dyadic), understood as a rhythm between a finite series or sequence, understood as spatially elaborated time, and what cannot be captured within its terms, the infinite. The point is not that nothing or no one dies. The point is only that living and dying punctuate an infinite series that no one can ever comprehend through a single or static idea. Consider his description of the Bacchanalian revel in the preface to *The Phenomenology of Spirit*. There he makes the point that what passes away in experience is essential to what is true. "The evanescent itself," he writes, "must, on the contrary, be regarded as essential, not as something fixed."[32] Eschewing the idea of "dead truth" that is concerned only with what can be determined as existing, Hegel seeks to establish the domain of appearance where it can be understood that "arising and passing away" does not itself arise and pass away but rather "constitutes the actuality and the movement of the life of truth." He writes that "the True is thus the Bacchanalian revel in which no member is not drunk; yet because each member collapses as soon as he drops out, the revel is just as much transparent and simple repose."[33]

Hegel lets us know in a separate fragment[34] that he seeks a condition in which "the infinite grief and whole gravity of the [spirit's] discord is acknowledged." Discord? Disquiet? Interestingly, the idea of an aesthetic form animated and animating is not one that overcomes negativity. It only works against the "deadening" effects of possession. To lose and to mourn requires giving up what we might think we possessed, which means giving up the fantasy that possession staves off transience. Sometimes mourning the loss of possession is the precondition of love itself, an initial undoing of a phantasm that makes way for something living. This is doubtless also why there may well be something enlivening in grief that is precisely the inverse of what is deadened by property and so has become as dead as property. And though in melancholy, one clings to the lost objects of the lost one, animating the one who is gone or dead, such animating powers indirectly testify to a persistent aliveness in the midst of loss.

Infinity, if there is one, is thus found rustling among the abandoned clothes and old stuff accidentally bequeathed by the dead—no one's property anymore—the rags, recycled, that eventually, perhaps, get taken up by some other body, in some other movement, evanescent and alive.

Kierkegaard's Speculative Despair

Every movement of infinity is carried out through passion, and no reflection can
produce a movement. This is the continual leap in existence that explains the movement,
whereas mediation is a chimera, which in Hegel is supposed to explain everything and
which is also the only thing he never has tried to explain.
—Kierkegaard, *Fear and Trembling*

Kierkegaard's critique of Hegel concerns primarily the failure of a philosophy of reflection to take account of what exceeds reflection itself:
passion, existence, faith. The irony in Kierkegaard's challenge to Hegelianism is, however, minimally twofold. On the one hand, Kierkegaard
will ask, where is it that Hegel, the existing individual, stands in relation to the systematic totality that Hegel elucidates? If for Hegel the
individual is outside the complete system, then there is an "outside"
to that system, which is to say that the system is not as exhaustively
descriptive and explanatory as it claims to be. Paradoxically, the very
existence of Hegel, the existing philosopher, effectively—one might
say *rhetorically*—undermines what appears to be the most important
claim in that philosophy, the claim to provide a comprehensive account
of knowledge and reality. On the other hand, Kierkegaard's counter to
Hegel consists in the valorization of passion and existence over reflection and, finally, language. It is in relation to this criticism that a different sort of irony emerges, one that Kierkegaard appears not to know,

but that attends his various claims to be writing on behalf of what is beyond speculation, reflection, and language. If Kierkegaard is right that Hegel omits the existing individual from his system, it does not follow that Kierkegaard maintains an unsystematic or nonspeculative view of the existing individual. Although Kierkegaard sometimes uses the speculative terminology of Hegelianism, he appears to parody that discourse in order to reveal its constitutive contradictions. And yet, in Kierkegaard's descriptions of despair in *Sickness unto Death* (1849), his use of Hegelian language works not only to displace the authority of Hegel, but also to make use of Hegelianism for an analysis that both extends and exceeds the properly Hegelian purview. In this sense, Kierkegaard *opposes* himself to Hegel, but this is a vital opposition, a determining opposition, one might almost say "a Hegelian opposition," even if it is one that Hegel himself could not have fully anticipated. If Hegel's individual is implicated in the very existence that he seeks to overcome through rationality, Kierkegaard constructs his notion of the individual at the very limits of the speculative discourse that he seeks to oppose. This appears to be one ironic way, then, that Kierkegaard's own philosophical exercise is implicated in the tradition of German Idealism.

Despair and the Failure to Achieve Identity

In the following, I will try to make clear why *despair* is a category, or, in Kierkegaard's terms, a sickness and a passion, whose analysis is crucial to both the extension and critique of Hegel in Kierkegaard's work. Insofar as despair characterizes the failure of a self fully to know or to become itself, a failure to become self-identical, an interrupted relation, then despair is precisely what thwarts the possibility of a fully mediated subject in Hegel's sense. That subject is documented in Hegel's *Phenomenology of Spirit* as an emerging set of syntheses, the subject as one who mediates and hence overcomes what initially appears as *different from itself*. The success of this mediating activity confirms the capacity of the subject to achieve self-identity, that is, to know itself, to become at home in otherness, to discover that in a less than obvious and simple way, it *is* what it incessantly encounters as outside of itself.

Hegel narrates in *The Phenomenology of Spirit* the various ways in which this mediating relation can fail, but insofar as Hegel claims that subject is substance, he defends the ideal possibility of articulating the *successful mediation* of each and every subject with its countervailing world. The various failures to mediate that relation effectively are only and always instructive; they furnish knowledge that leads to more effective proposals for how to mediate that apparent difference. Each time the subject in *The Phenomenology of Spirit* claims to discover the condition by which the mediating relation works, it learns that it has failed to take into account some crucial dimension of itself or of the world that it seeks to bind together in a synthetic unity. What it has failed to comprehend returns to haunt and undermine the mediating relation it has just articulated. But what remained outside the relation is always recuperated by the subject's synthesizing project: there is no final or constitutive failure to mediate. Every failure delineates a new and more synthetic task for the emerging subject of reflection. In a sense, Kierkegaard enters Hegel's system at the end of the *Phenomenology*: if Hegel thought that the subject of the *Phenomenology* had taken account of everything along the way that turned out to be outside the terms to be mediated, understanding *what* needed to be synthesized, as well as how that synthesis could take place, then the last laugh is on Hegel's subject. In its mania for synthesis, the subject has forgotten to include what can never be systematized, what thwarts and resists reflection, namely, its very existence and its constitutive and mutually exclusive passions: faith and despair.

In Kierkegaard's view, despair is precisely that passion that can never be "synthesized" by the Hegelian subject.[1] In fact, despair is defined by Kierkegaard as "a misrelation,"[2] one that confirms the failure of any final mediation and therefore signals the decisive limit to the comprehensive claims of the philosophy of reflection. Despair not only disrupts that subject's efforts to become at home with itself in the world, but it confirms the fundamental impossibility of ever achieving the self's sense of belonging to its world. The Hegelian project is not only thwarted by despair, but it is *articulated in despair* (*"the category of totality inheres in and belongs to the despairing person"*).[3] As we will see, one form of despair is marked by the effort to become the ground or origin of one's own existence and the synthetic relation to alterity. A kind of arrogance or hubris, this conceit of the Hegelian project suffers a humiliation at Kierkegaard's hands. To posture as a radically self-generated being, to be the author of one's will and knowledge, is to deny that one is constituted in and by what is infinitely larger than the human individual. Kierkegaard will call this larger than human source of all things human "God" or "the infinite." To deny that one is constituted in what is larger than oneself is, for Kierkegaard, to be in a kind of despair. Toward the end of this essay, we will consider just how crucial this form of despair is for Kierkegaard's own authorship. Indeed, it may turn out that the despair that Kierkegaard diagnoses in *Sickness unto Death*, and that in part he attributes to Hegel, conditions essentially the very writing whose object it is to denounce and overcome despair.

So despair is a "misrelation," a failure to mediate, but what are the terms to be mediated? And if Hegel fails to understand (his own) despair in the system he articulates, is it also true that Kierkegaard fails to understand the speculative conceptualization that inheres in the very notion of despair by which he counters speculation?

The opening page of *Sickness unto Death* appears to be a properly Hegelian exegesis populated with familiar terminology: "self," "spirit," "mediation," "relation." And yet, as the first paragraph proceeds, it becomes clear that Kierkegaard is parodying Hegel's language; significantly, however, this is a parody that does not entail a thorough rejection of Hegel. On the contrary, through parodying Hegel, Kierkegaard both recirculates or preserves some aspects of Hegel's system and jettisons some others. Parody functions like the Hegelian operation of *Aufhebung*, set into motion this time, ironically, by Kierkegaard to preserve, cancel, and also transcend the Hegelian corpus itself. The crucial dimension of *synthesis* is, of course, absent from this Kierkegaardian redeployment of Hegel. Parody functions for Kierkegaard as an *Aufhebung* that leads not to synthesis between his position and Hegel's, but to a decisive break. Kierkegaard does not lay out his arguments against Hegel in propositional form. He reenacts those arguments through the rhetorical construction of his text. If the issues he has with Hegel could be *rationally* decided, then Hegel would have won from the start. Kierkegaard's texts counter Hegel most effectively at the level of style, for part of what he wants to communicate is the limits of language to comprehend what constitutes the individual. Let us, then, consider the way in which this argument is performed through the parodic reiteration of Hegel at the outset of *Sickness unto Death*.

Kierkegaard begins part one of this text with a set of assertions and counterassertions, splitting his own philosophical voice into dialogic interlocutors, miming the dialectical style that dates back to Socrates: "A human being is spirit. But what is spirit? Spirit is the self. But what is the self?"[4] Then comes a ponderous sentence that one might expect to encounter at the hilarious limits of rationality in a Woody Allen film: "The self is a relation that relates itself to itself or is the relation's relating itself to itself in the relation; the self is not the relation but is the relation's relating itself to itself." The first part of the sentence is a disjunction, but it is unclear whether the disjunctive "or" operates to separate alternative definitions or whether it implies that the definitions that it separates are essentially equivalent to one another. Prior to the semicolon, there appear to be two definitions: one, the self is a reflexive relation (the self is what takes itself as its own object), and two, the self is *the activity* of its own reflexivity (it is that process of taking itself as its object, incessantly self-referential). If this is a Hegelian exposition, then one expects that this self will achieve harmony with itself, but here, it seems that the more the possibility of a synthesis is elaborated, the less likely that synthesis appears.

In the above quotation, then, we might ask: Can the self both be the relation and the activity of *relating*? Can the differently tensed definitions be reconciled? Is the first a static conception and the second a dynamic and temporalized one that is incompatible with the second? Or will we learn, Hegelian style, that the static notion is *aufgehoben* in the second, that the temporalized version of the reflexive self presupposes, transforms, and transcends the static one? After the semicolon, the sentence appears to contradict the definition of the self as static relation and to affirm the temporalized version of the self, thereby undermining the possibility of an emerging synthesis between the two versions: "the self is not the relation but is the relation's relating itself to the self." The original ambiguity over whether the "or" functions to set up a mutually exclusive set of alternatives or a set of appositional and equivalent definitions appears temporarily to be resolved into the first alternative.

The development of the sentence echoes the narrative logic of Hegel's *Phenomenology*, but in that text, it is more often the case that mutually exclusive alternatives are *first* laid out only then to be synthesized as part of a larger unity. Already in Kierkegaard's style of exposition, we see how the expectation of a Hegelian logic is both produced and undermined. Indeed, as the paragraph proceeds, that failure to conform to Hegelian logic turns into a full-blown illogic, a kind of high philosophical comedy. The rest of the paragraph reads as follows: "A human being is a synthesis of the infinite and the finite, of the temporal and the eternal, of freedom and necessity, in short, a synthesis. A synthesis is a relation between two. Considered in this way, a human being is still not a self."

Here the development of what appears to be an argument takes several illogical turns and seems by the propelling force of rationality to be spiraling into irrationality. By the end of the first sentence, we have concluded (a) that the self is temporalized, (b) that it is the *activity* of relating, and (c) that it is *not* a static relation. The possibility of a synthesis is therefore negated. This next sentence, however, poses as a logical consequence, but only to make a mockery of logical transition. Here we have the sudden and unwarranted shift from a discussion of the "self" to that of the "human being," and the announcement that the human being is a synthesis. Moreover, the terms of which that synthesis is composed are in no way implied by the static / temporal opposition that preoccupied the preceding sentence. Instead, we find wild generalizations asserted at once in the mode of a conclusion and a premise. As a conclusion that follows from the earlier sentence, this second sentence makes no sense. As a premise, it is equally absurd: the synthesis is asserted and described, and then the appearance of a conclusion emerges, "in short, a synthesis," which can be read only as a flagrant and laughable redundancy.[5] A didactic sentence follows, which is itself nothing other than a repetition of the obvious: "a synthesis is a relation between two." And then a most curious sentence concludes the paragraph in which Kierkegaard appears to take distance from the Hegelian voice that he has both assumed and mocked. "Considered in this way," the sentence begins, suggesting that there might be another way, Kierkegaard's way, "a human being is still not a self." Here Kierkegaard offers a distinction to suggest that what is called "the human being" is not the same as the self. But interestingly, we are also recalled to the problem of the temporality and tense of the self. What is described as the human being is "still not a self," not yet a self, a self that has not yet been articulated, or rather cannot be articulated within the language of synthesis.

Kierkegaard proceeds to take issue with this self that seems never to coincide with itself. He remarks that any synthesis requires a third term. The second and third paragraphs proceed in a note of tentative seriousness, making use of a Hegelian schematic precisely in order to show the way beyond it. The second paragraph begins: "In the relation between two, the relation is the third as a negative unity, and the two relate to the relation and in the relation to the relation." The examples of the terms to be related are the "psychical and the physical" in this textual instance. Kierkegaard argues that if the self is a synthesis of psychical and physical dimensions, and if it is *also* the activity of relating its psychical aspect to its physical aspect, then that very act of relating will have to be composed of one of those aspects. Here he assumes that the activity of "relating," a term that seems to have been kept purposefully abstract in the previous discussion, calls now to be specified as a psychical activity. This more specific determination of that relating activity will become even more significant as Kierkegaard's text proceeds to distinguish between *reflection*, the Hegelian way of understanding that constitutive relation, and *faith*, Kierkegaard's preferred way. As this semi-Hegelian exposition proceeds, Kierkegaard will show what is concretely at stake for the existing individual in this abstract logic.

Kierkegaard begins here to confound the distinction between the self as a static relation and the self as a temporal or active one. The two dimensions of the self to be related must already in some sense *be* the very relation, which is to say that psychical and the physical, as parts of the relation, are definitionally related, that is, presupposed as related, and are constantly in the activity of becoming relating. These two dimensions of that relation cannot be captured by a logic of non-contradiction. The reflexivity of this relation is what marks the relation as a self. For it is the distinguishing feature of a self to endeavor to become itself, constantly and paradoxically to be in the process of becoming what it already is. For one can always refuse to "relate" to oneself, to endeavor to become a self, but even then, that very refusal will still be a way of relating to the self. To deny that one has a self, to refuse to become one: these are not only modes of reflexivity, but specific forms of despair.

This paradoxical view of the self as what incessantly becomes what it already is coincides partially with Hegel's view of the subject. Hegel argues that the subject of the *Phenomenology* will develop and become increasingly synthetic, including all that it discovers outside itself in and as the world. And this subject, which successively appears to be identified as life, consciousness, self-consciousness, Spirit, Reason, and Absolute Knowledge, discovers finally that *implicitly* it has always been what it has become. The *becoming* of the Hegelian subject is the process of articulating or rendering explicit the implicit relations that constitute that subject. In this sense, the Hegelian subject is successively discovering what it has always already been, but has not known that it has been. The development or constitution of the Hegelian subject is the process of coming know what it is that that subject already is.

For Kierkegaard, however, this view of the subject is only partially true. For Hegel, the subject is every aspect of this relation: the subject is itself, the activity of relating, and that to which it relates (since the world, or Substance, turns out to be synthetically unified with the subject). It is precisely this circle of immanence, however, that Kierkegaard tries to break; he performs this break, however, by working Hegel's own logic to its own breaking point. A new paragraph following the above exposition graphically enacts the break with the Hegelian argument. Kierkegaard states an either / or question that cannot be asked within the Hegelian framework: "Such a relation that relates itself to itself, a self, must either have established itself or have been established by another." Here Kierkegaard raises the question of the genesis of this relation. It is not enough to know what the relation constitutes, nor to know that in some way it constitutes itself. The question remains: What has constituted this relation as a self-constituting relation? What put this circular relation into motion? Kierkegaard infers that there must be a relation that is temporally prior to the self-constituting self, that this prior relation must be reflexive and constituting, as well, and that the self must be one constituted product of that prior relation. This prior relation appears to be God, although Kierkegaard almost never supplies a definition of God.

Passionate Selves and the Affirmation of Faith

In *Concluding Unscientific Postscript* (1846), Kierkegaard makes clear that he is not interested in proving rationally that God exists, but only in the question of how to achieve faith as it arises for the existing individual: How do I become a Christian, what relation can I have to faith?[6]

If what constitutes the self remains part of that self, then the self whose task it is to take itself as its own object will of necessity take that prior ground of its own existence as its object, as well.[7] It is in this sense that for Kierkegaard, the self that takes itself as its own object will of necessity take "another" as its object, as well. In Hegel, this same formulation applies, but the "other" who constitutes the self will be the social other, the community of other subjects who collectively supply the common social and historical world from which the particular subject is derived. That move, however, is for Kierkegaard symptomatic of a refusal to see what transcends the social and human world, namely, the transcendent or the infinite from which the social world in its concreteness is derived.

The task of the self, for Kierkegaard, is indissolubly twofold: self-constituting, yet derived, the self is "a relation that relates itself to itself and in relating itself to itself relates itself to another."[8] Insofar as "another" is infinite, and this prior infinity constitutes the self, the self partakes of infinity, as well. But the self is also determined, embodied, and hence finite, which means that every particular self is both infinite and finite and that it lives this paradox without resolution. Faith will be described by Kierkegaard as infinite inwardness, the unceasing and passionate affirmation of the infinite, and in this sense, faith will be an occasion for infinity to emerge within the self: "that which unites all human life is passion, and faith is a passion."[9] In yet another sense, that self, however capable of infinite faith, will never be equivalent to the infinity that is prior to the individual, which Kierkegaard calls "God," but which is sometimes figured in terms of infinite possibility.[10] However infinite in its passion and faith, the self is still *existing*, and hence finite. Strictly speaking, the infinity prior to the self, the infinity from which the self emerges, does not *exist*. For un-actualized and infinite possibility to exist, it would have to become actualized, which is to become finite and hence no longer to be defin-able as infinite possibility. This infinite possibility, this ground or God, cannot be known or affirmed as a finite object, but can be af-firmed only by a passionate faith that emerges at the very limits of what is knowable.

This is an affirmation that cannot take place through rationality, language, or speculation; it emerges as a passion and a possibility only on the condition that reflection has failed. In Kierkegaard's *Philosophi-cal Fragments* (1844), he refers to this crisis in speculative thought as "the passion of Reason" and "the passion in all thinking."[11] Here, passion carries the meaning of suffering and longing, and Kierkegaard appears to imply that passion is generated precisely at the moment in which thought fails to grasp its object. Because part of what is meant by com-prehending an object is comprehending its origin and because that ori-gin or ground is the infinity of God, every act of knowing is haunted by the problem of faith, and hence also by passion. Kierkegaard com-mentator Niels Thulstrup describes this passion as "something which reason cannot comprehend and which leads reason to founder in its passion, the passion which wills the collision, which strives to discover that which cannot be thought and cannot be comprehended in the cat-egories of human thought."[12] In the face of the infinite, thought can supply only a finite concept or a word, but both of these are finitizing instruments that can only misconstrue and, indeed, *negate* what they seek to affirm. This is, of course, also the problem with Hegel's reli-ance on the concept to grasp infinity.[13]

One might be tempted here to think that Kierkegaard proposes that the self overcome its finitude in order to affirm through passionate inwardness the infinity from which that self emerges. But that is, for Kierkegaard, an impossibility. And here is where he appears to take Hegel seriously, even as he finally disputes him: the self is inevitably both finitude and infinitude, which the self lives, not as a synthesis, and not as the transcendence of the one over the other, but as a perpetual paradox. Inasmuch as the self is self-constituting, that is, has as its task the becoming of itself, it is finite: it is *this* self, and not some other. Inasmuch as the self is derived, a possibility actualized from an infinite source of possibility, and retains that infinity within itself as the passionate inwardness of faith, then that self is infinite. But to reconcile existence and faith, that is, to be an existing individual who, in its finitude, can sustain itself in infinite faith, that is the paradox of existence, one that can only be lived, but never overcome. As Kierkegaard puts it with characteristic irony: "to be in existence is always a somewhat embarrassing situation."[14]

Let us return then to the sentence from *Sickness unto Death* that suggests that the Hegelian subject, reconceived as a self (with the capacity for inwardness) and understood as derived from an infinite source, is both self-constituting and derived, "a relation that relates itself to itself and in relating itself to itself relates itself to another." This sentence, which appears logical and to some extent implicitly theological, leads to the introduction of despair as a psychological category: "This is why there can be two forms of despair in the strict sense. If a human self had established itself, then there could be only one form: not to will to be oneself, to will to do away with oneself, but there could not be the form: in despair to will to be oneself."[15]

Despair is the result of the effort to overcome or solve the paradox of human existence. If one seeks to be grounded in the infinite and to deny that one exists and is, therefore, finite, one falls into the despair of the infinite, willing not to be the particular self that one is. But if one denies the infinite and seeks to take full responsibility for one's own existence, viewing all of one's self as one's own radical creation, that is the despair of the finite.[16] It is this second form of despair, the despair of willing to be oneself, that is, to be the ground or sole source of one's own existence, that is more fundamental than the first. This second form constitutes a refusal to be grounded in what is more infinite than the human self and so constitutes a defiance of God. The primary way in which human selves fall into despair is through the repudiation of their infinite origins. This despair is marked by a certain hubris or arrogance and, at its limit, becomes demonic, understood as a willful defiance of the divine. We will consider that demonic extreme of despair toward the end of our remarks when we consider Kierkegaard's ambivalent relationship to his own authorship.

What this means, of course, is that if one knows one is in despair and seeks *by one's own means* to extricate oneself from despair, one will only become more fully steeped in that despair. That self is still trying to refuse its groundedness in what is greater than itself. Paradoxically, the self that refuses the infinite must enact that refusal *infinitely*, thereby recapitulating and reaffirming the infinite in a negative way in the very gesture of disbelief. If Hegel thought that the subject might be a synthesis of finite and infinite, he failed to consider that that subject, reconceived as a self with inwardness, can never mediate the absolutely qualitative difference between what is finite in that self and what is infinite. This failure of mediation is what underscores the paradoxical character of existence; the passionate and nonrational affirmation of that paradox, an affirmation that must be infinitely repeated, *is faith*; the effort preemptively to resolve this paradox is the feat of despair. In this sense, despair marks the limit of dialectical mediation, or rather every effort at mediation will be read by Kierkegaard as symptomatic of despair. Every synthesis presumes and institutes a *repudiation* of what cannot be comprehended by thought; infinity is precisely what eludes conceptualization. That refused infinity returns, however, as the infinite movement of despair in the existing individual who seeks to resolve the paradox of existence through thought. Through the invocation of despair, Kierkegaard marks out the limits of the Hegelian ideal of synthesis: "Despair is the misrelation in the relation of a synthesis that relates itself to itself."[17]

The Hegelian ideal of becoming at one with oneself is achieved through one's social relations and through one's relation to everything that is outside the self. For Hegel, the subject discovers that other human beings and objects are part of its own identity, that in *relating* to others and to objects, the human subject enacts (or actualizes) some of its own most fundamental capacities. Hence, the subject achieves a certain oneness with itself through relating to what is different from itself. This oneness, however, is not a possibility for the Kierkegaardian self. As much as that self might want to affirm itself as the ground or origin of its own relations with others, it is bound to fail. This self can take responsibility for its own capacities by denying that it is itself produced by what is greater than itself. That is one kind of despair, the despair of willing to be oneself. On the other hand, if that self tries to relinquish all responsibility for itself by claiming that some greater and infinite reality, God, has produced everything about that self, then that self is in a different kind of despair, the despair of willing not to be oneself. There is no escape from this paradox. Hence, to be a self means either to be in one of these two forms of despair or to have faith. But in both despair and faith, this paradox is never resolved. In despair, one lives one side of the paradox and then another (one takes radical responsibility for oneself or not at all), but in faith, one affirms the paradox, taking responsibility for oneself at the same time affirming that one is not the origin of one's existence.

One might ask, is one always either in despair or faith? The answer for Kierkegaard is yes. For the most part, human beings live in despair, and they do not even know that they are in despair. In fact, this not knowing that one is in despair is a symptom of despair. The person who does not know that there is a task, a struggle to affirm oneself in this paradoxical way, makes some set of presumptions about the solidity of its own existence that remain unquestioned and hence outside the difficulty of faith. And there appears to be no way to faith except through despair. But faith for Kierkegaard does not provide a solution for the paradox of the self. Indeed, nothing provides such a solution. The self is an alternation, a constant pitching to and fro, a lived paradox, and faith does not halt or resolve that alternation into a harmonious or synthetic whole; on the contrary, faith is precisely the affirmation that *there can be no resolution*. And insofar as "synthesis" represents the rational resolution of the paradox, and the paradox cannot be resolved, then it follows that faith emerges precisely at the moment at which "synthesis" shows itself to be a false solution. This is, as it were, Kierkegaard's last laugh on Hegel. Whereas Hegel argues that the failure of any given synthesis points the way to a greater and more inclusive synthesis, Kierkegaard tries to show that synthesis itself, no matter how inclusive, cannot resolve the paradox of the self. Concretely, this difference between Hegel and Kierkegaard implies that the self will ultimately have a very different experience of and in the world. For Hegel, the subject will eventually find a unified and harmonious relation with what appears at first to be outside itself, so that it can, ideally, find itself at home in the world, "of" the world that it is "in." But for Kierkegaard, what is "outside" the finite self, namely, the infinite, is also "within" the self as freedom and the dual possibility of despair and faith (all of which are "infinite" passions, passions that can have no end); further, the infinite that persists as the ground of the finite self or within the self as its own passion will never fully belong to the finite self or the finite world in which it nevertheless exists in some less than apparent way. Hence, for Kierkegaard, the infinity that is the source of the self and that persists in the self as its passion will never fully be "of" the world in which it dwells. The self, for Kierkegaard, will be perpetually estranged not only from itself, but from its origins and from the world in which it finds itself.

One might imagine a Hegelian rejoinder to Kierkegaard's affirmation of the paradoxical self. Hegel might argue that if there is something in the self that is infinite, that infinity must nevertheless *appear* in some way in order to be *known*. In Hegelian language, one might say that for the infinite to become actual and hence knowable, it must become determinate or appear in some form. And Hegel imagined that certain kinds of concepts could be both finite (particular, determinate, specific) and infinite (nonspecific, indeterminate, unbounded). Hegel wanted to arrive at a concept, understood as a kind of speculative thought, in which the finite and the infinite would not only coexist, but be essentially dependent on one another. Imagine a thought that would be *your* thought, specifically yours, and therefore determined and specific, but that would *at the same time* be a thought of what is infinite and hence not bound to you at all, indeed, not bounded or limited by anything. Hegel imagined that the thought of the infinite depends on the determinate thinker, the place and existence of that thinker, at the same time that that infinite thought exceeds that determinate place and thinker. In this sense, the infinite thought depends on the finite thinker in order to be thought, in order to have its occasion and its form, and the finite thinker is no thinker, that is, is not really thinking, thinking thought through to its infinite possibility, unless that finite thinker is able to think the infinite. Hence, for Hegel, a mutual dependency exists between what is finite and what is infinite in the human subject, where both the finite and the infinite form the project of thinking.

Kierkegaard's rejoinder is firm. If one tries to *think* the infinite, one has *already* made the infinite finite. There can be no thinking of the infinite, for the infinite is precisely not only what cannot be thought, but what insistently forces a crisis in thought itself; the infinite is the limit of thinking, and not a possible content of any thought. To the Hegelian claim that the infinite must first *appear* before it can be known, Kierkegaard would have to respond that the infinite can neither appear nor be known. Hence, it is to some extent *against* Hegel that Kierkegaard formulates his notion of the infinite and, therefore, also of faith: the infinite eludes the dialectic, the infinite cannot be grasped or "understood" by any rational effort of thought or synthesis. The infinite can be affirmed nonrationally and hence passionately, at the limits of thought, that is, at the limits of Hegelianism.

Fear, Trembling, and Other Inward Passions

This opposition to Hegel puts Kierkegaard in a bind, for Kierkegaard is *a writer*; he puts his opposition to Hegel into words, and he produces concrete and determinate texts, finite things that house his claims about what is infinite. How do we understand Kierkegaard, the finite man or "existing individual," in relation to this notion of the infinite, which can never fully be expressed by any finite or determinate statement or text. As finite expressions, Kierkegaard's own texts, *Sickness unto Death* itself or *Fear and Trembling* (1843), can only *fail* to express the very notion of infinity that they seek to communicate. Whereas a Hegelian might argue that Kierkegaard's writing of the infinite is itself essential to the infinite that it expresses, Kierkegaard's response will be that if there is an infinite that can never be resolved with the finite, then Kierkegaard's own texts will always *fail* to communicate the infinite. Indeed, Kierkegaard's response will be: "My texts *must* fail to express the infinite, and it will be by virtue of that *failure* that the infinite will be affirmed. Moreover, that affirming of the infinite will not take the form of a thought; it will take place at the limits of thought itself; it will force a crisis in thought, the advent of passion."

So for Kierkegaard to set about to write a book against Hegel, against synthesis, and in favor of passion and faith, he must write a book that fails to communicate directly the very passion and faith he seeks to defend. An author cannot embody or express the infinite, for that "expression" would inadvertently render finite what must remain infinite. Indeed, the words "passion" and "faith" cannot express or communicate passion and faith; they can only *fail* to communicate and in failing *point the way* to an affirmation that is fundamentally beyond language. Aware of this paradoxical task of trying to write about what cannot be delivered in language, Kierkegaard insists upon the necessity of indirect communication, a kind of communication that knows its own limitations and by enacting those limits indirectly points the way to what cannot be communicated.

Evidence of Kierkegaard's views on indirect communication can be found in the fact that he often wrote and published under a pseudonym. *Sickness unto Death* was published with "Anti-Climacus" as its author. *Fear and Trembling* was written by "Johannes de Silentio" and

Philosophical Fragments by "Johannes Climacus," also the author of *Concluding Unscientific Postscript*. Other pseudonyms include "Constantin Constantius" (*Repetition*, 1843) and "Victor Eremita" (*Either / Or*, 1843). The use of a pseudonym raises the question who is the author behind the author? Why is Kierkegaard hiding? What is it that is concealed in this writing, and what is it that is revealed? Does the author mean to say what he says, or does the pseudonymous author allow the "real" author to write what he would not write under his own name. What does it mean to write under the name of another? I do not want to suggest that pseudonymous authorship always works in the same way or for the same reasons in Kierkegaard's work. But it does seem directly related to the problem of writing the infinite that we mentioned above. The false name suggests that whatever is written under that name does not exhaust the full range of what the author, Kierkegaard, might be. Something is not being uttered or expressed or made known. Minimally, it is Kierkegaard the man who to some degree hides behind the fictional author under whose name he writes. On an existential level, however, there is something in every self that *cannot be expressed* by any act of writing. There is that in every self that is silent, and Kierkegaard is clear that in the end, faith, and passion more generally, are not matters of writing or speaking, but of remaining silent.

If Kierkegaard's texts, then, are to be works of faith, they must not only be labors of language, but labors of silence, as well. This is suggested by the pseudonym "Johannes de Silentio," the "author" of *Fear and Trembling*. And in that text, we encounter the figure of Abraham, whose silence cannot be understood by the author. Indeed, Abraham stands for faith; he is called "a knight of faith," and yet he does not speak and leaves us no clues by which we might be able to find reason in his faith. The author tries repeatedly to understand Abraham's faith, but fails.

What is the story of Abraham, and what is the nature of Abraham's faith? Abraham receives a sign from God that he is to take his son to the top of a mountain, Mount Moriah, and there to slay his son as an act of faith. According to the Bible, Abraham does not tell Isaac, his son, what he is about to do, and neither does he tell Sarah, his wife. Through the pseudonym of Johannes de Silentio, Kierkegaard opens *Fear and Trembling* by telling the story of Abraham several times. Each effort to narrate what happened with Abraham is also an effort to fathom how it is that Abraham could prepare himself to act in such a way. If Abraham were willing to slay his son, he risks becoming a murderer, according to conventional ethical norms; he destroys his own son, his own family, breaking the most cherished of *human* bonds. Johannes de Silentio tries to fathom how it could be that Abraham, who loved his son, was nevertheless willing to defy, resist, or suspend that love as well as one of the most fundamental laws of ethics in order to perform his faith. What kind of faith has God exacted from Abraham such that he must prepare himself to sacrifice that worldly connection that is most important to him. Is this a cruel God, one to be disobeyed? And why does Abraham persist in his course, silently bringing Isaac to the top of Mount Moriah and raising his hand, only *then* to have his hand stayed by God?

The example is, of course, a shocking one, but Kierkegaard rehearses that scene of Abraham climbing Mount Moriah, drawing the sword, and he tries to understand how any human being could turn against what is most important to him in the world. Abraham supplies no explanation, and Kierkegaard leads us to the point of understanding that there can be no explanation in words. In the name of what? For what higher good? For Johannes de Silentio, the answer never comes, but the questions repeat themselves insistently, exhausting language and opening out into the silent void of faith.

Kierkegaard imagines how it would be for Abraham to feel the full force of his love for Isaac and at the same time follow the dictates of a faith that requires the sacrifice of Isaac. This is surely a paradox, and in the story of Abraham, we receive from Kierkegaard something like an allegory of the paradoxical self. There is no way to reconcile the profoundly finite and worldly love of a father for his son with a notion of faith that is infinite, "in" the world, but not "of" it. This is precisely the kind of paradox that cannot be thought, cannot be resolved into some harmonious solution, but that wrecks thought, forces an exposure of thought itself. In Kierkegaard's indirect words: "I cannot think myself into Abraham"; "For my part, I presumably can describe the movements of faith, but I cannot make them"; "faith begins precisely where thought stops."[18]

But Kierkegaard is not only horrified by the sacrifice that faith has exacted from Abraham. He is also appalled by the fact that Abraham appears to get Isaac back, that God not only asks for a sacrifice, but returns what has been lost, and all this *without reason*. Furthermore, it appears that Abraham does not turn against the God who has, it seemed, played so cruelly with the most precious object of Abraham's human love: "to be able to lose one's understanding and along with it everything finite, for which it is the stockbroker, and then to win the very same finitude again by virtue of the absurd—this appalls me, but that does not make me say it [faith] is something inferior, since, on the contrary, it is the one and only marvel."[19]

On the one hand, Kierkegaard is appalled by the *arbitrariness* and whimsical character of the way in which God is figured here as giving and taking away. On the other hand, Abraham's faith is a marvel, since it does not waver in the face of the alternating beneficence and cruelty of this ultimate authority. Abraham is not shrewd with respect to God. Abraham does not figure that if he only acts as if he is willing to sacrifice Isaac, God will stay his hand: "he had faith by virtue of the absurd, for all human calculation ceased long ago."[20] If faith designates the limit of thought, if faith emerges precisely when thought fails to comprehend what is before it, then Abraham climbs the mountain and draws the sword *without knowing* that God will return Isaac to him. What is awesome in Abraham is that he sustains his faith *without knowing* that he will receive Isaac back. Faith is not a bargain; it is that affirmation that emerges when all bargaining has failed. This is what Kierkegaard means when he claims that Abraham has faith by virtue of the absurd. And if faith is a leap, it is a leap beyond thought, beyond calculation, a leap made from and with *passion* that can be neither comprehended by thought nor communicated through language.

In *Fear and Trembling*, Kierkegaard claims that he cannot yet make this leap, but that he can only trace its steps and applaud that movement as a marvelous thing. He knows enough to recognize that Abraham must have been in anxiety at the moment in which he drew that sword. And whereas there are those who would defy God and return to the ethical world, refuse to draw the sword, and allay their anxiety in that way, Abraham is not one of them. And whereas there are those who would turn against their love for Isaac and deny the importance of that bond, Abraham is not one of them. He turns against neither the finite (Isaac) nor the infinite (God), but prepares for the paradoxical affirmation of both. In preparing to sacrifice Isaac, however, Abraham performs "the teleological suspension of the ethical."[21] This is not the denial of ethics, but the suspension or postponement of the ethical domain in the name of what is higher, namely, the infinite or the divine. The human and finite world is grounded in what is larger than itself, namely, the infinite, and there are occasions in which the affirmation of that infinity takes priority over the affirmation of the finite and ethical domain that is the product of that infinity. But this suspension of the ethical entails anxiety, and faith does not resolve anxiety, but exists with it. Any finite individual can have faith only by contracting anxiety, for all faith involves some loss or weakening of worldly connections, including the worldly connection to one's own finite, bodily self. There is in faith a dying away of the finite self, this body, this name, these worldly connections to family, friends, lovers, this belonging to a time and a landscape, a home, a city. Faith underscores that all those finite things in which we are invested are perishable and that there is no necessary reason or assurance that they will remain as we know them or survive at all.

If the story of Abraham is an allegory of faith, and if Abraham himself is a figure for faith, then we can read the story for its more general philosophical implications. Aristotle once claimed that philosophy begins with a sense of wonder, the wonder that there are things, rather than no things. Aristotle's "wonder" is not so different from Kierkegaard's sense of the marvelous in his encounter with Abraham's faith. For Aristotle, wonder emerges over the fact *that* there are things, not over *how* things came about—although that interested him, too—but that things came about at all. Kierkegaard writes of "the emotion which is the passionate sense for coming into existence: wonder."[22] In Kierkegaard's terms, it is, on the one hand, a marvel that these specific finite beings, humans, the elements, objects of all kinds, came into the world, rather than some other set of beings. On the other hand, it is terrifying that all that exists appears to come into the world for no necessary reason at all. For if there is no necessary reason that things came into the world, there is no necessary reason that sustains those very things in the world, and there is no necessary reason that keeps those things from passing out of the finite world. If these finite beings came into the world from a set of infinite possibilities, then why is it that of all the myriad and countless beings that came into the world, *these* came into being? There appears to be no necessity that *these* beings came into existence and that others did not, if we consider that the source or origin of all things is infinite possibility, another name for God. But the wonder or marvel is provoked by another realization, as well. If what exists in the finite realm is the actualization of a set of possibilities, and this set of possibilities is only a subset of the infinite possibilities that are not actualized in the existing world, then how do we account for which possibilities made the *passage* from infinite possibility into what exists in the finite world? No reason can be supplied: there is no necessity for what exists to exist. In fact, not only is there no necessity for the infinite, God, to create the finite, the human world, but it is perfectly absurd that he did at all.

The finite is grounded in the infinite: we know this from Kierkegaard's analysis of despair. But the finite never fully expresses the infinite that is its origin. Precisely to the extent that an existing individual, for instance, is finite, that is, limited, mortal, located in space and time, and bodily, that individual is clearly not infinite, and hence does not fully express the infinity out of which he or she (absurdly) arises. This passage from the infinite to the finite cannot be thought; it is wondrous and a marvel, but also quite terrifying, for there is no necessary reason for anything to exist, or, for that matter, to persist in its existence, that is, to stay alive. Whatever God is for Kierkegaard, "he" (Kierkegaard tends not to personify God) is not what supplies a reason or a necessity for what exists. On the contrary, the postulation of the Kierkegaardian God underscores that existence itself is absurd.

The story of Abraham suggests that whatever exists in this world does so by virtue of a kind of grace, an arbitrary and irrational act. Existence can be understood as a kind of unexpected gift, one that comes just as easily as it is taken away. To have faith means to affirm this contingency, this absurd coming into being of existence, regardless of the suffering that recognition of absurdity causes. To transform the terror produced by the recognition of existence in its absurdity is no easy task. Indeed, the aesthete and the ethicist cannot find relief from this terror; they are in despair to the extent that they are run by this terror and involved in sensuous or ethical endeavors that seek to quell the anxiety produced by the fact of human contingency. The knight of resignation in *Fear and Trembling* can be understood as a figure at the limit of the ethical domain, tracing the movements of faith, but not able to make the necessary leap. As a consequence, he is *horrified* by the prospect of Abraham's "sacrifice" of his own son; indeed, the knight of infinite resignation can understand Abraham's intended act as a murder—and not a sacrifice or offering to God.

We might then understand the movement from the ethical domain to that of faith as the transformation of terror into a sense of grace. The difficulty with making this movement, however, is that the prospect of losing one's worldly attachments, indeed, one's own finite existence for no necessary reason, is not easy to face with anything other than terror. Kierkegaard understood that the task of faith would be especially difficult to accomplish by those who lived according to the romantic impulse to invest existing individuals with such enormous value that they cannot imagine themselves continuing to exist in a world without them. This was the anguished predicament of the young man in *Repetition*, and there is good evidence to support the view that Kierkegaard himself felt just this way about Regine Olsen, with whom he broke off an engagement to be married. This broken engagement can be understood as Kierkegaard's own "sacrifice," which, from an ethical point of view, appeared to be the emotional equivalent of murder.

In the midst of Kierkegaard's discussion of Abraham's faith in *Fear and Trembling*, he remarks with due irony that if Hegel's philosophy were right, then Abraham would indeed be a murderer. For Kierkegaard, Hegel represents the ethical domain, for in Hegel's *Phenomenology of Spirit* and *Philosophy of Right*, he argues that the individual realizes his or her true and proper purpose in a community bound by *ethical* laws. Indeed, Hegel argues that if an individual holds himself or herself to be above the ethical law, that individual is sinful. Kierkegaard objects to Hegel's characterization of the assertion of individuality as sin. According to Kierkegaard, Hegel fails to understand that the individual is higher than the universal ethical norm, that there are times when ethical laws must be "suspended" or "surrendered" so that a higher value can be affirmed, namely, the value of faith—which, of course, for Kierkegaard, is always an *individual* affair. The relation to God cannot be mediated. (This belief aligns Kierkegaard with Luther.) Hegel would believe that God is present in the ethical law and that individuals, by submitting to the ethical law, come into a mediated relationship to God. This happy reconciliation of the ethical (called "the universal") and the religious (called "the absolute") is one that Kierkegaard firmly rejects. The middle term, the ethical or "universal," which Hegel understands to mediate between the individual, on the one hand, and the divine, on the other, is for Kierkegaard precisely what must be subordinated and suspended for the absolute and immediate relation of faith to become animated between the individual and God: "this position cannot be mediated, for all mediation takes place only by virtue of the universal; it is and as such remains for all eternity a paradox, impervious to thought."[23]

In Kierkegaard's view, Hegel's ethical community requires the sacrifice of the individual to an anonymous law. As law-abiding citizens, we are interchangeable with one another; each of us expresses our true and proper self through the same acts by which we conform to a law that applies to all human beings, regardless of our differences. In this sense, none of us are individuals before the law, or rather each of us is treated by the law as an anonymous subject. Insofar as Abraham takes distance from the ethical law that prohibits murder, he becomes an individual, and the more he refuses to honor the authority of that law over his own existence, the more individuated he becomes. This act of putting into question the ethical law as a final authority over one's life engages Abraham in anxiety, for in questioning the law, Abraham encounters his own being apart from the ethical community in which he stands.

Opposing himself to Hegel's notion of individuality as sin, Kierkegaard values this anxiety as human freedom, the demand to make a decision whether or not to comply with the law or whether to follow a higher authority. Although Hegel appears to worry about such a moment in which the individual stands apart from the ethical community, suspending the power of its laws to govern his or her life, Hegel also appreciates fear and trembling as necessary moments in the development of the human subject.[24] Significantly, Kierkegaard does not acknowledge that moment in Hegel in which fear and trembling are considered to be necessary experiences in the acquisition of human freedom. We can find that moment at the end of Hegel's well-known chapter in the *Phenomenology* entitled "Lordship and Bondage." There, the bondsman who has been the property of the lord has cut himself loose from his own enslavement. What we might expect is the jubilant celebration of freedom, but what we encounter in the emerging bondsman instead is a shattering fear. Consider the following description of the emancipated bondsman from Hegel's *Phenomenology of Spirit* as an example of the fear and trembling produced by the experience of human freedom temporarily untethered by authority. The bondsman labors on objects, and for the first time *recognizes* his own labor in what he makes. In the recognition of *himself* in the object of his making, he is struck with fear: "the formative activity . . . has the negative significance of *fear*. For, in fashioning the thing, the bondsman's own negativity [his freedom] becomes an object for him . . . this objective *negative* moment is none other than the alien being before which it has trembled."[25]

Whereas the bondsman has been afraid of the lord, he is now frightened of his own freedom, now that that freedom has become what "lords" over his own existence. A few lines later, Hegel continues with a passage that further links the expression of freedom through work with the experience of fear:

> Without the formative activity, fear remains inward and mute, and consciousness does not become explicitly *for itself*. If consciousness fashions the thing without that initial absolute fear, it is only an empty self-centered attitude. . . . If it has not experienced absolute fear but only some lesser dread, the negative being has remained for it something external [its freedom still appears to belong to another and is not yet its own], its substance has not been infected by it through and through.[26]

Hegel goes on to remark that if the bondsman has not been shaken by fear in the very fiber of its being, it will remain "a freedom enmeshed in servitude."

We can begin to see here that Kierkegaard's characterization of Hegel is not always fair. Hegel is clearly not in favor of the enslavement of the individual to the ethical law, for the fear and trembling associated with the moment of emancipation will inform the individual as he or she enters ethical life in the following chapter in the *Phenomenology*. Indeed, one might well ask the question of whether Kierkegaard's very language of "fear and trembling" is not derived from Hegel's description of the emerging bondsman in *The Phenomenology of Spirit*. How far is the bondsman's trembling at the sight of his own freedom from Abraham's anxiety in the face of his own potential act? How do these "tremblings" differ?

Whereas Hegel's bondsman trembles before what he has created, the external confirmation of his own power to create, Abraham trembles (inwardly) before what he is compelled by God to sacrifice and destroy. Whereas the bondsman is frightened of his own capacity to create, a capacity that in its apparent limitlessness makes the bondsman into a figure with enormous responsibility and power, Abraham is compelled to act according to a divine demand that he cannot understand. In this sense, Abraham's freedom is not guided by reason, but by what is irrational, beyond reason, and that requires an obedience to that irrationality over any human law. The bondsman, on the other hand, appears to legislate a law for itself, expressed in its own "formative activity" or labor. The bondsman appears to be temporarily without an authority, a "lord," who is other to himself. But Abraham, he is enthralled to a Lord who is so radically different from himself that he cannot understand him at all. That the bondsman is compelled to be free without the guidance of a supervening authority is an unbearable situation that leads to the development, in the following chapter on the "Unhappy Consciousness," of a *conscience*, the self-imposition of an ethical law, what Hegel himself understands as a form of self-enslavement. Hence, Hegel's bondsman retreats from the fearful prospect of his own freedom through enslaving himself to ethical projects and practicing various rituals of self-denial. Abraham, on the other hand, must bind himself to an authority whose demands are incomprehensible, an act that leaves him frighteningly detached from the ethical community and from his own rational capacities. Kierkegaard tells us that it is through this persistence in fear and trembling that Abraham comes to the full and gracious experience of faith.

The task of faith is to continue to affirm infinite possibility in the face of events that appear to make existence itself a radically impossible venture. What astonished Kierkegaard about the Abraham story is that Abraham faced the prospect of losing what was most precious to him in the world, and he still did not lose faith and curse God: he maintained his faith not only in the face of that loss, but in the face of having to make the sacrifice himself.[27] Abraham loves Isaac, but that human bond cannot be the most important passion of his life, for what merely exists can come and go, and that transience can never be the object of faith. If in the throes of romantic love or in the complicated emotional ties of family life we say that our existence is meaningless without some existing individual, that is a symptom that we are in despair. For Kierkegaard, if any existing individual becomes the fundamental reason to live, that individual must be sacrificed so that faith can return to its proper object: the infinite.

In *Repetition*, published simultaneously with *Fear and Trembling*, Kierkegaard relates the story of how a young man, a thinly veiled substitute for Kierkegaard himself, breaks off an engagement with a girl he loves. The sacrifice appears absurd, for he has not fallen out of love with her. And yet if the girl has become the ultimate reason for living, the source of all affirmation, then the young man has transferred and invested the boundlessness of his passion onto an existing individual: this is, for Kierkegaard, a kind of despair and a failure of faith. Precisely because she has become an object he is not willing to lose, he must demonstrate his willingness to lose her altogether. His sacrifice is not unlike Abraham's, except that Abraham, being a "knight of faith," receives Isaac back again, whereas the young man, a veritable "knight of resignation," appears to orchestrate and suffer an irreversible loss. He knows how to sacrifice finite things and to avoid the despair that characterizes the life of the aesthete, as well as the ethicist, but he does not know how to affirm that infinity that appears to make existence utterly absurd.

What does it mean that whereas Abraham receives Isaac back, the young man in *Repetition* fails to have his love returned? To have faith means no longer to invest absolute meaning in what is finite, whether it is an individual person, a set of objects or possessions, a homeland, a job, a family. All of these sites of investment are finite and perishable, and when we transfer religious passion onto those things, according to Kierkegaard, we turn away from God and invest the things of this world with a displaced religious meaning and hence fall into despair. If one makes the leap of faith, then one invests absolute passion and meaning in the infinite; this entails a suspension not only of the ethical, but of the finite realm altogether, for any finite object of passion will now be understood as emerging as a gift from the infinite and passing back eventually into the infinite. For Kierkegaard, it is only once we affirm the transience and contingency (nonnecessity) of what we love in this world that we are free to love it at all. If Abraham gets Isaac back, it is because he has suspended his attachments to what is finite, affirmed the infinite, and so understood that nothing that exists in this world can sustain an absolute passion. It is in this sense that Isaac was always a gift from God; one's own existence is a gift, and that of every other existing thing.

Of course, to recognize that there is no necessary reason that some beings exist and other possible beings do not produces not only a sense of wonder, but a sense of terror, as well. The thought of an existing life as a contingency, as an arbitrary event that just as well could not have happened or that could without reason pass away, this is a thought that, strictly speaking, cannot be maintained; it is a thought that founders on itself, for how can a thought think the contingency of the thinker who thinks it? But it is this thought that leads to the anxiety over existence that leads to the question of faith. To witness the existing world this way, as a terrifying and wondrous gift, is to know that one is not the author of that world, that the father, strictly speaking, is not the "origin" of the son, and that not only do all things originate—

absurdly, wondrously—in the infinite, but all existing things return there, as well.

For Kierkegaard, this problem of the contingency of existence has implications for human love, a passion that verges on faith, but that becomes despair when it becomes too much like faith, an absolute or infinite passion. To love what exists without at the same time knowing the fragile and contingent nature of existence is to be in despair; if one tries to love a human object as if it were absolute, one projects a religious passion onto a human object. The result, for Kierkegaard, is to become wracked with displaced passion and a constant sense of loss. Kierkegaard describes this problem at some length in the first volume of *Either / Or.* Considered to be part of Kierkegaard's early writings, *Either / Or* is composed of two volumes. The first offers writings that enact and explore the aesthetic point of view; the second volume offers sermons and treatises in the ethical point of view. Neither of these perspectives is the same as faith, but Kierkegaard, in unmistakenly Hegelian fashion, suggests that these two spheres, these two ways of approaching the world, have to be experienced in order to understand the limits of each and the superiority of faith. There is no writing in the perspective of faith in either of these volumes, but it is unclear that such a writing could exist; faith is nevertheless there in the writings as the path not chosen, the way to affirm the paradox that emerges between the aesthetic and ethical perspectives.

The vain effort to make of a human being an object of absolute and infinite passion is the fateful predicament of the aesthete in *Either / Or.* The alternative in that text is to become a purely ethical being, one who makes no attachments to anything finite, but acts in accordance with a universal law, a law that applies to everyone and that makes of its obedient subject an anonymous and impersonal subject. The aesthete, on the other hand, values what is most immediate and finite as if it were absolute; the ethical person (also termed the "knight of infinite resignation") treats the human law as if it were absolute and invests his or her full passion into the application of that law. The one in faith, however, lives fully in the finite world, but affirms its contingency at the same time. This is the marvel that Kierkegaard claims he cannot perform, to love what exists and to affirm that it might be lost, that it cannot serve as the ultimate object of passion, that for which one lives. Human love requires the knowledge of grace, that what is given for us to love is not ours and that its loss refers us to what is the origin of all things finite, including ourselves. This means that for the one who has faith, love is always an anxious and ironic affair, and there is no way to see directly how that infinite faith in what is infinite lives alongside the finite love of what exists. In Kierkegaard's terms, "absolutely to express the sublime in the pedestrian—only that the knight [of faith] can do it, and this is the one and only marvel."[28]

One implication of Kierkegaard's paradoxical view of faith is that it is not a form of asceticism. Kierkegaard does not advise a turning away from the finite world. On the contrary, he imagines that the knight of faith will be one who dwells among the ordinary world of things, a "tax collector," he suggests in *Fear and Trembling*. One would not be able to see from the outside that this individual has faith, for faith, by virtue of its radical inwardness, is inexpressible. The entirety of the finite realm would be "returned" to such an individual for the paradoxical reason that through faith, he or she no longer fears the loss of what exists; in faith, the individual affirms the absurdity and arbitrariness by which the existing world comes into being and passes out again. That affirmation is not a kind of wisdom or knowledge, but an irrational passion that emerges at the limits of all thinking.

The Paradoxical Language of Faith

Although it is clear that Kierkegaard writes in favor of faith, there are at least two remaining questions that trouble any reader of his works. The first question concerns the "what" of faith: In what does Kierkegaard have faith? What is this God that appears to be the infinite, or, more specifically, infinite possibility? The second question is intimately related to the first: How could we have received an answer to the question "In what does Kierkegaard have faith?" if we expect the answer to arrive *in language*? After all, we have already learned that faith cannot be expressed in language, that it is the infinite passion of the inwardness of the self. But what is the status of Kierkegaard's own texts, if we understand the purpose of these texts to be an incitement to faith? How do these texts work? How do they achieve their purpose, if from the start, we know that they can never express faith, or, if they claim to have expressed faith, they have failed in that very task?

Kierkegaard's God is infinite which means that this God can never be identified with one of his products. This God is said to be the origin of the existing world, but this is not a God who, in a personified form, at some point in history—or prior to history—said "Let there be light," and light suddenly there was. And it is not that Kierkegaard disputes the truth of the Bible, but he insists that the truth of the Bible is not to be found in the language of the text. In this sense, Kierkegaard is against a literal reading of the Bible, one that takes every word printed there to be the transmitted word of God. On the contrary, the "truth" of the Bible is not, properly speaking, *in* the text, but is to be found *in the reader*, in the various acts by which the various injunctions to faith are *appropriated* and taken up by those who read the text. The truth of the Bible is to be found in the faith of those who read the Bible. The text is a *condition* by which a certain kind of instruction in faith takes place, but faith can never be achieved by learning what the Bible says, only by finally turning away from that text and turning inward to discover the infinite passion that emerges from the demand to affirm contingency. In *Philosophical Fragments*, the Bible and biblical scholarship are treated with irony: these texts can deliver no *historical* truth of interest to the person interested in faith, for no historical documentation regarding the existence or teachings of Jesus Christ can ever convince a person into faith. Faith does not arrive as the result of a persuasive argument; faith (along with its alternative,

despair) is precisely what has the chance to emerge when all argu-
mentation and historical proof fail.[29]

But there is a further difficulty with a historical approach to faith.
Some Christian scholars argue that it can be proven that Jesus Christ
lived, that he came into the world, and that he was the son of God.
The proof "that" he existed is, however, not enough for Kierkegaard.
That assertion simply prompts him to ask a series of philosophical
questions that the historical enquiry cannot answer: What does it mean
for anything to "come into existence"? If something can be said to
"come into existence," then at some early point in time, it did not exist at all. How, then, can something that is nonbeing become transformed into being? This is, of course, the question that preoccupied
us above when we considered how philosophical wonder focuses on
the apparent absurdity that some things exist, rather than not, that
certain possibilities become actual or finite, whereas other possibilities remain merely possible. Possibility and actuality are mutually exclusive states, that is, a thing is either possible or actual, but it would
make no sense to say that it is both at once. Therefore, to say that a
given thing has come into existence implies that it has moved from a
state of possibility to one of actuality. This transition cannot be
"thought," says Kierkegaard, but is a contradiction, one that accompanies all "coming into being."

In *Philosophical Fragments*, Kierkegaard considers the highly significant paradox that in the person of the Savior (whose historical status
remains uncertain, or at least irrelevant), it appears that what is eternal has come into time and that what is infinite has appeared in finite
form. Whereas Hegel would claim that the finite appearance in this
consequential instance expresses and actualizes the infinite, that this
person in time, aging and mortal, expressed what can never die, Kierkegaard takes issue with such a notion, arguing that this occur-
rence is utterly paradoxical, that the human and divine aspects of the
figure of Christ can never be reconciled; insofar as he is infinite, he
cannot appear in finite form without losing his status as infinite; and

insofar as he is finite, he cannot become infinite, for finitude implies mortality.

What is striking about Kierkegaard's writing in *Philosophical Fragments* is that the so-called miracle of God coming into existence recurs at every moment that some finite thing "comes into being." Christ is no exception to this paradoxical movement, but neither is he singular. After all, every human self emerges from a set of infinite possibilities and so moves from the infinite (which is nonbeing, what is not yet finite and does not yet have a specified kind of being) to the finite (or being). Indeed, anything that comes into existence is miraculous for the very reasons we set out above in our discussion of wonder. In making this move, Kierkegaard appears to be taking an almost arrogant distance from the church authorities, the scriptures, and the religious authorities whose task it is to settle historical details about Christ's sojourn on earth. Indeed, Kierkegaard goes so far as to subject the key concepts of Christianity to a new set of definitions, ones that are devised by him. Kierkegaard is not interested in testing his interpretations against the Bible or against earlier interpretations; he devises and sets forth his own. Throughout the introductory chapter of *Philosophical Fragments*, Kierkegaard appears to take over the power to name that properly belonged to God in the book of Genesis. In Genesis, God spoke and said, "Let there be . . . light, man, woman, beasts, etc.," and the very power of his voice was sufficient to bring these entities into being. Kierkegaard appears to appropriate this power of naming for himself, but the entities he brings into existence through his writings are Christian concepts. As a result, he *names* these concepts and, in the naming, revises their meaning according to his own interpretive scheme: "What now shall we call such a Teacher, who restores the lost condition and gives the learner the Truth? Let us call him *Saviour* . . . let us call him *Redeemer*." Further definitions are offered for "conversion," "repentance," "New Birth," and more.[30]

What are we to make of this Kierkegaardian willingness to fabricate new meanings for the orthodox terms of Christianity? Is it not a kind of arrogance or pride to offer new interpretations for such words? By what right does Kierkegaard proceed with such obvious enthusiasm to create new meanings for old words? Is this creative way with words related to Kierkegaard's enigmatic career as an author?

What is the authority of the author? For Kierkegaard, faith cannot be communicated, so that any effort to write a book that communicates faith will, by definition, have to fail. In this way, then, Kierkegaard must write a book that constantly fails to communicate faith, a book that insistently renounces its own authority to state what faith is, a text that turns back upon itself and effectively wills its own failure. If the reader of his book knows that the book cannot offer knowledge of faith, then that reader will be seduced by the promise of that knowledge only, to be disappointed in an instructive way. Kierkegaard's language must, then, perform the paradoxical task of enacting the limits of language itself. The author who wishes to point the way to faith must resist every effort to communicate faith directly; in other words, that author must will the failure of his own book, and in that very failure know its success.

In *Sickness unto Death*, Kierkegaard considers the peculiar kind of despair that afflicts "poets" and makers of fiction. We can read in this diagnosis a thinly veiled autobiographical confession. Consider that Kierkegaard is a kind of poet,[31] one who produces a fictional narrator for most of his early texts through the construction of various pseudonyms. He then produces "examples" of faith and despair, fabricating "types" of individuals, embellishing on biblical and classical characters: Abraham, Don Juan, etc. And now consider Kierkegaard's diagnosis of the person who suffers from defiant despair, the will to be oneself, that is, the will to be the sole ground and power of one's own existence and therefore to take the place of God: "this is the self that a person in despair wills to be, severing the self from any relation to a power that has established it, or severing it from the idea that there is such a power . . . the self in despair wants to be master of itself or to create itself."[32]

Kierkegaard then explains that this kind of despairing individual regularly fantasizes that he or she is all kinds of things that they are not: "the self in despair . . . constantly relates to itself only by way of imaginary constructions."[33] This fiction-producing self can make itself into "an imaginatively constructed God," but this self is for that reason "always building castles in the sky . . . only shadowboxing."[34] At an extreme, this defiant form of despair becomes *demonic* despair, and here, the will to fabricate and fictionalize asserts itself in clear defiance, even hatred, of God. Is there, for Kierkegaard, a stark opposition between the life of faith and that of fiction making? And can Kierkegaard himself give up his imaginary constructions in order to live the life of faith, one that we know, from the consideration of Abraham, is a life of silence?

Demonic despair, which Kierkegaard calls the most intensive form of despair, is rooted in "a hatred of existence": "not even in defiance or defiantly does it will to be itself, but for spite."[35] And what evidence does such a person have against existence? The one in demonic despair is himself the evidence that justifies his hatred of existence. This appears to imply that the one in demonic despair, that incessant maker of fictions, *hates himself* for producing an imaginary construction of himself, but nevertheless persists in this self-fabrication. This is a self that, through fiction making, postures as the creator of its own existence, thus denying the place of God as the true author of human existence. But this demonic self must also despise itself for trying to take over the power of God. This self in demonic despair alternates between self-fabrication and self-hatred. Inasmuch as this demonic one is an author, and is Kierkegaard himself, he produces a fiction only then to tear down the construction he has just made. The one in demonic despair can acknowledge the divine authorship that enables his own fiction, his pseudonymous work, only by admitting that what he has produced is a necessary fraud.

At the end of part one of *Sickness unto Death*, Kierkegaard appears to begin this disavowal of his own production, clearing the way for an appreciation of God as the only "first-rate author" in town, acknowledging that Kierkegaard's own work must always be understood as derived from the power that constitutes him, a power that precedes and enables his own imaginary production:

> Figuratively speaking, it is as if an error slipped into an author's writing and the error became conscious of itself as an error—perhaps it actually was not a mistake but in a much higher sense an essential part of the whole production—and now this error wants to mutiny against the author, out of hatred toward him, forbidding him to correct it and in maniacal defiance saying to him: No, I refuse to be erased; I will stand as a witness against you, a witness that you are a second-rate author.[36]

Written in 1848 and published in 1849, the text shows us Kierkegaard's evolving intention to resist the seduction of authorship. Two years earlier, he wrote in his journal: "My idea is to give up being an author (which I can only be altogether or not at all) and prepare myself to be a pastor."[37] It appears that Kierkegaard gave up his career as a literary and philosophical author after *Sickness unto Death* and persevered in writing purely religious tracts. Had he achieved faith? Did he overcome despair? Was his writing as compelling after the leap, or did it turn out to require the very despair he sought to overcome?

Sexual Difference as a Question of Ethics

Alterities of the Flesh in Irigaray and Merleau-Ponty

Although Luce Irigaray's *An Ethics of Sexual Difference* is a feminist reading of selected philosophical works, we should perhaps not be so clear about what that means. Feminist in an unfamiliar sense, her text is not primarily a criticism of how various philosophers have represented women, and it is not a philosophy offered from a feminist or a feminine point of view. It is, I would suggest, a complex engagement with philosophical texts, one that in the first instance appears to accept the terms of the texts, as evidenced by the lengthy and elaborated citations from those texts. In this sense, then, one might at first glance conclude that by virtue of these profuse citations, Irigaray seeks to make herself accountable to the texts that she reads; indeed, one might even conclude that there is a certain self-subordination in the way that she foregrounds again and again passages from the male philosophers that she reads.

But the way in which she cites from these texts suggests a different kind of relation, neither a simple subordination nor a simple practice of mockery or derision. Indeed, I want to suggest that in her very practice of citation, Irigaray enacts an ambivalent relation to the power attributed to these texts, a power that she at once attributes to them, but also seeks to undo. What is perhaps most paradoxical and enigmatic about her textual entanglement with these texts, and with Merleau-Ponty's in particular, is that it enacts and allegorizes the kind of entanglement—or intertwining—that characterizes relations of flesh. In this sense, then, the text enacts the theory of flesh that it also interrogates, installing itself in a hermeneutic circularity from which it cannot break free and in whose hold it appears quite willfully to stay.

Irigaray's reading of Merleau-Ponty's "The Intertwining" is in many ways quite dismissive and contemptuous, attributing to him an arrested development, a maternal fixation, even an intrauterine fantasy. And yet her dependency on his theorization of tactile, visual, and linguistic relations seems absolute. There is no thinking outside his terms, and hence there is always an attempt to think about his terms. This involves her in a spectacular double bind: thinking against him within his terms, attempting, that is, to exploit the terms that she also seeks to turn against him in an effort to open the space of sexual difference that she believes his text seeks to erase.

Consider the implication of her strategy of writing for both the implicit relations of power that hold between the two writers and the theory of the flesh that appears to be both thematized and enacted in the intertwined reading that Irigaray performs. First, her presumption is that his discourse sets the terms by which the critique of that discourse becomes possible; second, the terms of his work also have, in her view, the power to constitute the intelligibility of bodies and the flesh; third, that constitutive power is based in a refusal of the feminine, in her terms, or an erasure and covering over of sexual difference; fourth, that Irigaray's miming and citing of his work are the exclusive ways in which his terms are exposed to failure; which means, fifth, that the power to counter his work is derived from the very work that is countered.

Whereas it might be plausible to conclude from the above that Irigaray, in countering the presumed power of Merleau-Ponty's essay, can only and always confirm and enhance that power, is it not possible to read that doubled reflection of his work in hers in a different way? Whereas one might be tempted to conclude that for Irigaray, the feminine is radically outside of dominant philosophical discourse and hence Merleau-Ponty's reflection on the flesh, or that, perhaps equivalently, power is exclusively located in that dominant discourse, the textual engagement that characterizes her reading suggests a more conflicted and ambivalent deployment of power, radically implicated in what it opposes, opposing the Other through a strange participation and consumption of his terms. Her position is distinct from a view in which the feminine is radically other and from phallogocentrism, which, radically itself, appropriates sexual difference. Irigaray textually enacts a kind of entanglement that suggests that the "outside" to phallogocentrism is to be found "within" its own terms, that the feminine is insinuated into the terms of phallogocentrism, rendering *equivocal* the question, *whose voice is it, masculine or feminine?* Significantly, then, the relation of power and the relation of the flesh, understood as allegorized by the textual relations that Irigaray draws from his text to hers, is not one of *opposition*, rallying the feminine against the masculine, but of exposing and producing a mutually constitutive relation. On the one hand, this means that the masculine is not being able to "be" without the "Other," that the repudiation of the feminine from phallogocentrism turns out to be the exclusion without which no phallogocentrism can survive, that is, the negative condition of possibility for the masculine. Conversely, Irigaray's miming of Merleau-Ponty's prose, her insinuation into his terms, not only proves the vulnerability of his terms to what they exclude, but exposes that vulnerability to what they exclude as a constitutive vulnerability. His text is disclosed as having her text intertwined within his terms, at which point his text is centered outside itself, implicated in what it excludes, and her text is nothing without his, radically dependent upon what it refuses.

In fact, I would suggest, in citing the texts as she does, she quite literally dislocates the philosophical tradition by relocating it within her own text; she does not refuse this tradition, but incorporates it, in some odd way, making it her own. But what, we might ask, happens to these texts by virtue of this strategy of citational appropriation? Do they remain the same, and if not, what is Irigaray telling us, what is she exemplifying, about how feminist philosophy should proceed in relation to the masculinism of the canon from which it is spawned? Can it be that her reading exemplifies an appropriation and refusal at once?

Before I propose what her answer to this question might be, I would like to underscore that one purpose that unifies this text, that recurs throughout these lectures, is the elaboration of what Irigaray will call the ethical relation between the sexes. The ethical relation between the sexes, she will argue, cannot be understood as an example of ethical relations in general; the generalized or universal account of ethical relations presumes that men and women encounter each other as subjects who are symmetrically positioned within language. This language, she argues, is not, however, neutral or indifferent to the question of sex; it is masculinist, not in the sense that it represents the contingent interests of men, but in the sense that it consistently disavows the identification of the universal with the masculine that it nevertheless performs. If language asserts its universality, then every specific disposition of language is subsumed under this postulated universality. Language becomes what not only unifies all specific dispositions, but, in Irigaray's view, what refuses to consider the salient distinction between the sexes as a difference that establishes different kinds of languages, a difference that contests the very notion of universality, or rather reveals that what has passed as universality is a tacit or unmarked masculinity. We might want to learn more about what Irigaray thinks is the characteristic mark of a masculinist use of language and what a feminine, but there are no "empirical languages" that correspond to the sexes; oddly, it seems, it is only this very pretension to be universal that characterizes the masculine, and it is this very contestation of the universal that characterizes the feminine. In other words, it is not that certain masculine values yet to be named are elevated to the status of the universal, but rather that whatever those values might be, their very elevation to the status of the universal, this tendency to universalization itself, is what constitutes the characteristically masculine. Conversely, this rupture or unassimilable difference that calls into question this universalizing movement is what constitutes the feminine in language; it exists, as it were, as a rupturing of the universal or what might be understood as a protest within the universal, the internal dissent of the feminine.

What precisely is meant by "the universal" in the above characterization? And what is its bearing on the ethical relation between the sexes that Irigaray imagines and promotes and that she understands to be central to the project of feminist philosophy? Let us remember that for Irigaray, to universalize a norm or to substitute oneself for another would be examples of an ethical procedure that presumes the symmetrical positioning of men and women within language. Indeed, if women and men were symmetrically or reciprocally positioned within language, then ethical reflection might well consist in imagining oneself in the place of the other and deriving a set of rules or practices on the basis of that imagined and imaginable substitution. But in the case that men and women are positioned *a*symmetrically, the act by which a man substitutes himself for a woman in the effort to achieve an imagined equality becomes an act by which a man extrapolates his own experience at the expense of that very woman. In this scenario, for Irigaray, the act by which a man substitutes himself for a woman becomes an act of appropriation and erasure; the ethical procedure of substitution thus reduces paradoxically to an act of domination. On the other hand, if from a subordinate position within language, a woman substitutes herself for a man, she imagines herself into a dominant position and sacrifices her sense of difference from the norm; in such a case, the act of substitution becomes an act of self-erasure or self-sacrifice.

One might well conclude that for Irigaray, given her view of the asymmetrical position of men and women in language, there can be no ethical relation. But here is where she offers a way of thinking about the ethical relation that marks an original contribution to ethical thinking, one that takes sexual difference as its point of departure. In her view, the ethical relation cannot be one of substantiality or reversibility. On the contrary, the ethical relation might be said to emerge between the sexes precisely at the moment in which a certain incommensurability between these two positions is recognized. I am not the same as the Other: I cannot use myself as the model by which to apprehend the Other: the Other is in a fundamental sense beyond me and in this sense the Other represents the limiting condition of myself. And further, this Other, who is not me, nevertheless defines me essentially by representing precisely what I cannot assimilate to myself, to what is already familiar to me.

What Irigaray will term masculinist will be this effort to return all Otherness to the self, to make sense of the Other only as a reflection of myself. This is what she will call the closed circuit of the subject, a relation to alterity that turns out to be no more than a reduction of alterity to the self. It is important to note that it is not only men whose relations are characterized by this closed circuit, by this foreclosure of alterity. The difference between "men" and masculinism is here at stake: when and where such a foreclosure takes place, it will be called "masculinist." Paradoxically, and we will see, consequentially, Irigaray will herself manifest the ability to identify with this position, to substitute herself for the masculinist position in which alterity is consistently refused, and she will mime that universal voice in which every enunciatory position within language is presumed to be equivalent, exchangeable, reversible. We might read the profusion of citations in her text as sympathetic efforts to put herself in the place of the Other, where the Other this time is a masculinist subject who seeks and finds in all alterity only himself. Oddly, in miming the masculinist texts of philosophy, she *puts herself in the place of the masculine* and thereby performs a kind of substitution, one she appears to criticize when it is performed by men. Is her substitution different from the one she criticizes?

Although readers who know Irigaray from *Speculum of the Other Woman* might expect that she will now turn and destroy this position, this masculinism, with a cutting edge, indeed, with a threatened castration, I would like to suggest that the exchange that she performs with the masculinist texts of philosophy in *An Ethics of Sexual Difference* is more ambivalent and less cutting than in that earlier text. Whereas the earlier text tended to underscore the way in which the feminine was always and relentlessly both excluded and presupposed in the theoretical constructions of both Plato and Freud, this later text does that, but also does something more. Here, she seems, paradoxically, to acknowledge her debt to those philosophical texts she reads and to engage them in a critical dialogue in which the very terms she uses to engage these texts critically are borrowed from these texts, or, one might say, borrowed against them. She is, as it were, locked in dialogue with these texts. The model for understanding this dialogic relation will not be one that presupposes simple equality and substitutability, nor will it be one that presupposes radical opposition. For let us remember that Luce Irigaray is a philosopher and is thus part of the enterprise she will subject to criticism; but she is also a feminist, and according to her view, that means that she represents precisely what has been excluded from philosophical discourse and its presumptions of universality.

Irigaray reads the final chapter of Merleau-Ponty's posthumously published *The Visible and the Invisible*, called "The Intertwining—the Chiasm," as an example of this monologic masculinism, even as it is a text from which she also clearly draws the philosophical means to offer an alternative way of approaching the ethical relation. Merleau-Ponty's text is one in which he considers how the philosophical effort to understand knowledge on the model of vision has underestimated the importance of tactility. Indeed, he will suggest that seeing might be understood as a kind of touching, and he also suggests that in the touch, we might be said to be "perceiving," and further, that touching or seeing something has a reflexive dimension and that the realm of the visible and the realm of the tactile imply each other logically, overlapping with each other, ontologically. His writing is filled with purposefully mixed metaphors in order to suggest that language, vision, and touch intertwine with each other and that aesthetic experience may be the place in which to investigate that synesthetic dimension of human knowledge. In the place of an epistemological model in which a knowing subject confronts a countervailing world, Merleau-Ponty calls into question that division between subject and world that conditions the questions characteristic of the epistemological enterprise. He seeks to understand what, if anything, brings the subject and its object into relation such that the epistemological question might first be posed.

In an argument that can be seen to extend Heidegger's effort in *Being and Time* to establish the priority of ontology to epistemology, Merleau-Ponty seeks to return to a relation that binds subject and object prior to their division, prior to their formation as oppositional and distinct terms. Heidegger insisted that every interrogative relation that we take toward an object presupposes that we are already in relation to that object, that we would not know what to ask about a given object if we were not already in a relation of affinity or knowingness about the object. In the introduction to *Being and Time*, Heidegger considers not only what it might mean to pose the question of the meaning of Being, but what might be derived, more generally, from an explanation of "what belongs to any question whatsoever." He prefigures for us what will come to be called the hermeneutic circle when he writes,

> all inquiry about something is somehow a questioning of something ... so, in addition to what is asked about, an inquiry *has that which is interrogated* [*ein Befrateges*] ... [and] what is asked about is determined and conceptualized. Furthermore, in what is asked about there lies also *that which is to be found out by the asking* [*das Erfragte*]. ...

Inquiry, as a kind of seeking, must be guided beforehand by what is sought. So the meaning of Being must already be available to us in some way.[1]

In this move whereby the question, the interrogative, is referred back to an already established and already available set of ontological interrelations, Heidegger seeks to show that the questions we pose as a subject of an object are themselves a sign that we have lost or forgotten some prior ontological connection to the object, which now appears to us as foreign and unknown. In Merleau-Ponty, a similar move takes place, but unlike the Heidegger of *Being and Time*, Merleau-Ponty will argue in *The Visible and the Invisible* that the web of relations that conditions every interrogative and that every interrogative might be said to forget or conceal is a *linguistic web*; sometimes he will use the term "mesh" or "weave," or even "interconnective tissue," but the implication is clear that it is a *binding* set of relations in which all apparent differences are superseded by the totality of language itself. Here one might say that Merleau-Ponty has transposed the problematic introduced by Heidegger as one in which ontology is shown to precede epistemology to the framework of structuralist linguistics in which language is said to precede epistemology in a restricted sense. By "epistemology" here, we mean only a set of questions that seek to know something that is not yet properly or adequately known. Like Heidegger, Merleau-Ponty's point is to try to overcome a subject-object distinction that he understands to be presupposed and reinforced by the epistemological tradition. The subject-object distinction presupposed and instituted through this tradition presupposes that the subject is ontologically distinct from its object, but it does not ask whether there might be some common substrate or genesis from which both subject and object emerge and that joins them in some original way.

Irigaray will enter this discussion with the following question: If every question presupposes a *totality* of already established relations, ones that are temporarily forgotten or concealed in the asking about something apparently unknown, what place is left for the asking of a question about what is not already known? The presumption of an already established totality of relations, whether they are conceived as ontological or linguistic, is symptomatic, in her view, of the self-circuit of the subject according to which every moment of alterity turns out to be presupposed by the subject, to be always already this subject, and hence not to constitute a moment of alterity at all. Indeed, the much touted "always already" that, in phenomenology, designates the prejudicative realm of taken for granted meanings would be paradigmatic of this kind of masculinist monologism in which alterity and the not yet known and not yet knowable are refused.

What, Irigaray effectively asks, do we make of the *never yet known,* the open future, the one that cannot be assimilated to a knowledge that is always and already presupposed? For Irigaray, the ethical relation will be represented by the question as an act of speech, the open question, the one that does not claim to know in advance the one to whom it is addressed, but seeks to know who that addressee is for the first time in the articulation of the question itself. In her words, the ethical relation consists in the question: "Who are you?" This is the question that seeks to cross the difference that divides masculine from feminine, but not to cross that difference through a substitution that presupposes the equivalence and interchangeability of masculine and feminine. "Who are you?" is the paradigmatic ethical question, for her, in the sense that it seeks to cross the divide of sexual difference, to know what is different, but to know it in such a way that what is different is not, through being known, assimilated or reduced to the one who seeks to know.

And yet this "ethical" dimension appears in some conflict with the textual strategy elucidated at the beginning of this chapter. In the "ethical" view, sexual difference is precisely an unfathomable and irretraversible difference constitutive of masculine and feminine in relation to one another. Their relation is considered on the model of the encounter, and the ethical problem they face is how best to approach, without assimilating, the Other. In her view, there is no masculine without a prior implication in the terms of the feminine, and there is no feminine without a prior implication in the terms of the masculine; each term admits to its own internal impossibility through its relation to the Other. The relation is not primarily that of an *encounter*, but rather of a constitutive intertwining, a dynamic differentiation in proximity.

A few difficulties emerge in relation to this way of circumscribing the ethical relation. It makes sense to ask whether Irigaray's focus on the ethical deflects her critical attention from the prior and constitutive relations of power by which ethical subjects and their encounters are produced. Open to challenge is the presumption that the question of alterity as it arises for ethics can be fully identified with the question of sexual difference. Clearly, problematic dimensions of alterity take a number of forms, and sexual difference—though distinct in some ways—is not the primary difference from which all other kinds of social differences are derivable. Regarded as an ethical question, the relation of sexual difference presumes that it is only the masculine and the feminine who come into an ethical encounter with the Other. Would one, within this vocabulary, be able to account for an ethical relation, an ethical question, between those of the same sex? Can there even be a relation of fundamental alterity between those of the same sex? I would of course answer yes, but I think that the peculiar nexus of psychoanalysis and structuralism within which Irigaray operates would be compelled to figure relations among women and among men as either overly identificatory or narcissistic and in that sense not yet of the order of the ethical. Must there be a difference between the sexes in order for there to be true alterity? Similarly, there are other sorts of social difference that distinguish interlocutors in language, and why is it that these social differences are considered somehow as less fundamental to the articulation of alterity in general and to the scene of the ethical in particular? Finally, is it not the case that Irigaray portrays the masculine, and Merleau-Ponty in particular, in ways that do not do justice to the ethical dimension of his own philosophical explorations in *The Visible and the Invisible?*

Rather than take these questions on their own terms, I suggest that we consider how the textual production of intertwinement calls into question the ethical framework that Irigaray defends. For what emerges between Irigaray and Merleau-Ponty is not "difference" per se, but a founding implication in the Other, a primary complicity with the Other without which no subject, no author, can emerge. And this situation poses an even more difficult "ethical" question than the one that Irigaray articulates: how to treat the Other well when the Other is never fully other, when one's own separateness is a function of one's dependency on the Other, when the difference between the Other and myself is, from the start, equivocal.

Taking this last question first, let us consider Merleau-Ponty's text in relation to Irigaray's "reading" and consider what in that text might resist the interpretation that she brings to it. Merleau-Ponty will be accused by Irigaray of a "labyrinthine solipsism." In support of this characterization, she calls attention to the following kind of argument that he makes. In relation to the phenomenological description of touch, Merleau-Ponty argues that one cannot touch without in some sense being touched by what one touches, and one cannot see without entering into a field of visibility in which the seer is also potentially, if not actually, seen. In both cases, there persists a relation of reversibility between what might be called the subject and object poles of experience. But there is, in addition to these two reversible relations, the one of touch and the one of sight, a crisscrossing of the two reversible relations. Consider the following citation from "The Intertwining—The Chiasm" in *The Visible and the Invisible:*

> It is the coiling over of the visible upon the seeing body, of the tangible upon the touching body, which is attested in particular when the body sees itself, touches itself seeing and touching the things, such that, simultaneously, *as* tangible it descends among them, *as*

touching it dominates them all and draws this relationship and even this double relationship from itself, by dehiscence or fission of its own mass.[2]

Merleau-Ponty is describing something like the unfolding and differentiation of the lived world of flesh, where flesh is understood not only as both agent and object of touch, but also as the ground or condition of seeing and the seen. In an important sense, this term "flesh" is what is being described by both the reversibility of touch and the reversibility of seeing, and it is what conditions and what is articulated by both reversibilities.

But what is this "flesh," and can it be said to be other than the articulations, differentiations, and reversibilities by which it is described? Is it the same as this set of reversible relations, or is it that with which Merleau-Ponty cannot finally come to terms? Irigaray will argue that in Merleau-Ponty's account, there is nothing outside the selfsame touching and touched body, seeing and seen, and that this closure attributed to the reversible relation constitutes its solipsism. Although this "flesh of the world" or "flesh of things" appears to designate some domain that encompasses and exceeds either pole of that reversible relation, the term remains obscure, and for Irigaray, the term works as a sign of that closure and hence in the service of a solipsism. For Irigaray, this is a central problem with Merleau-Ponty. She writes of such passages that "the subtlety of what is said of the visible and its relation to the flesh does not rule out the solipsistic character of this touch(ing) between the world and the subject, of this touch(ing) of the visible and the seer in the subject itself."[3]

Although Merleau-Ponty's formulation is meant to overcome the isolation of the seeing and touching subject and to argue that the subject, through its sight and touch, is implicated in and by the very world it explores, for Irigaray, the effect of his formulation is that the subject himself becomes extolled as that to which all worldly relations return. And yet, is her assessment fair? Consider that the phenomenological counter to Cartesianism that Merleau-Ponty articulates is in part a refusal of that perceptual distance postulated between the reflecting subject and the world of objects. In breaking apart this distinction, the perceiving "I" acquires a flesh that implicates him or her in a world of flesh. Hence, for Merleau-Ponty, the embodied status of the "I" is precisely what implicates the "I" in a fleshly world outside of itself, that is, in a world in which the "I" is no longer its own center or ground. Indeed, only upon the condition of this philosophical move toward a more embodied "I" does Irigaray's intervention becomes possible. Underscoring the dependency of that embodied "I" on a body prior to itself, Irigaray identifies the maternal body as the literal condition of possibility for the epistemic relation that holds between the embodied "I" and its embodied objects. Although Irigaray reads this primary and constituting "world of flesh" as a diffusion of the maternal, a deflection or refusal of the maternal, what is to secure the primacy of the maternal? But why reduce the world of flesh, the world of sensuously related significations, to the maternal body? Is that not an "appropriation" and "reduction" of a complex set of constituting interrelations that raises the counterquestion of whether Irigaray seeks to have "the maternal body" stand in for that more complex field? If one is "implicated" in the world that one sees, that does not mean that the world that one sees is reducible to oneself. It may mean quite the opposite, namely, that the "I" who sees is in some sense abandoned to the visible world, decentered in that world; that the "I" who touches is in some sense lost to the tactile world, never to regain itself completely; that the "I" who writes is possessed by a language whose meanings and effects are not originated in oneself.

Although Irigaray might be read as having "lost" herself to Merleau-Ponty's text in a similar way, it remains curious that the "ethical" model she invokes for understanding this relation appears to obscure this relation of primary implicatedness and the consequently equivocal status of sexual identity. The masculinism of this subject is never put into question by Irigaray. She will claim that it is the mark of the masculine to assimilate all alterity to the preexisting subject. But what makes this refusal of alterity, a refusal that takes the form of incorporating the Other as the same, a specifically masculine or masculinist enterprise? Here is where Irigaray's philosophical argument rests on a use of psychoanalytic theory in which the masculine is understood to be defined in a less than fully differentiated relationship to a maternal origin. The mother becomes for him the site of a narcissistic reflection of himself, and she is thus eclipsed as a site of alterity and reduced to the occasion for a narcissistic mirroring.

Irigaray accepts the psychoanalytic account that argues that the individuation of the masculine subject takes place through a repudiation of his maternal origins, a repudiation of the *in utero* bodily connection to the mother, as well as of the vital dependency on the mother in infancy. This break with the maternal is thus the condition of his becoming a masculine subject and the condition of his narcissism, which is, as it were, an appreciation of himself as a separated and bounded ego. In what is perhaps the least persuasive of Irigaray's arguments, she suggests that Merleau-Ponty not only repudiates this "connection" with the maternal in classic masculine fashion, but that he then reappropriates this "connection" for his own solipsistic theory of the flesh, which he describes as the "medium" or "connective tissue." In a sense, she reads his theory of the flesh as a philosophical transposition of the infant's connection with the maternal body, a repudiation of that connection and a return of the repudiated within his own philosophical text. She reads him as taking this "connective tissue" as what he, the masculine subject, occasions and what, far from connecting him with anything, returns him to a solipsistic circle of his own making. On the basis of this argument, Irigaray then concludes that for Merleau-Ponty, there is no connection with what is not the subject, with what is different, with the feminine, and hence with alterity in general.

But if one refuses to accept Irigaray's account of the formation of masculine narcissism through the repudiation of the maternal, her argument becomes more difficult to support. If one refuses, as well, the thesis that sexual difference is the key or decisive index by which relations of alterity are established and known, and, further, refuses to accept the easy transposition of a psychoanalytic account of masculine narcissism into a philosophical account of solipsism, then her position becomes increasingly untenable.

But let us consider what is, after all, most important about Irigaray's contribution to the thinking of the ethical relation here, namely, the claim that a relation of substitutability between masculine and feminine constitutes a kind of appropriation and erasure and the call for some other kind of ethical relation, interrogative in structure and tone, that marks an open relation to an Other who is not yet known. Irigaray considers the complex interrelations in Merleau-Ponty's account of language, sight, and touch to amount to a masculine solipsism. We will follow her reading here, but not merely to show what she means and how she comes to support what she means. For it will be shown, I hope, that Irigaray is more implicated in the text she criticizes than she herself concedes and that, considered rhetorically, her text avows the availability of Merleau-Ponty's text to a feminist appropriation and hence stands in an unintended dialogic relation to Irigaray, even as she accuses that text of being closed to dialogue.

The argument Irigaray makes against Merleau-Ponty proceeds in the following way: to claim, as he does, that the relation of touch or sight is reversible is to claim that the one who touches can be touched, the one who sees can be seen, and that the subject and object poles of these experiences are bound together by a connective "flesh of things." This reversibility presupposes the substitutability of the subject pole with the object pole, and this substitutability, she argues, establishes the *identity* of both toucher and touched, seer and seen. ("The reversibility of the *world* and *I* suggests," she writes, "some repetition of a prenatal sojourn where the universe and I form a closed economy.")[4]

But remember that there is a relationship between these two reversible relations, between touch and sight, and that that relationship is not fully reversible. Of this relation, Irigaray reiterates Merleau-Ponty's position with some measure of apparent sympathy:

> Of course there is a relation of the visible and the tangible. Is the doubling redoubled and crisscrossed? This is less certain. The look cannot take up the tangible. Thus I never see that *in which* I touch or am touched. What is at play in the caress does not see itself. The in-between, the middle, *the medium* of the caress does not see itself. In the same way and differently, I do not see what allows me to see. . . . This is perhaps, as far as I am concerned, what Merleau-Ponty calls the site of flesh in which things bathe?[5]

Hence, there is something that conditions the reversibility of these relations, that is itself not reversible, an enabling condition that persists as a kind of substratum, indeed, a *hypokeimenon*, without which no visibility or tactility would exist. And it seems to be the selfsame substratum that conditions the reversibility of tactile relations and visible ones and that in neither case can be fully touched or fully seen.

Of what is this substratum composed? Irigaray will, in a predictably psychoanalytic way, read this flesh out of which all sensate experience is composed as the flesh of the maternal, and as in her reading of the *Timaeus*, she will suggest that this unnameable substrate is the repudiated maternal itself. In this sense, the feminine might be said to condition masculine solipsism, understood as the closed circuit of those reversible relations; but what conditions them is what must be excluded from them, their defining limit, their constitutive outside. Excluded, unnameable, but a necessary precondition, the feminine resides metaphysically as the diffuse "flesh of things." But here, as before, it seems crucial to ask whether it is appropriate to "correct" this diffusion and to reassert the primacy of the maternal or to question instead this putative primacy. After all, the maternal body is situated in relations of alterity without which it could not exist, and these relations, strictly speaking, precede and condition the maternal body (indeed, often, such relations, understood as norms, restrict certain bodies from becoming "maternal" bodies altogether). The "flesh of the world" in its very generality refuses the synecdochal collapse by which all sensuousness becomes reduced to the maternal as the sign of its origin. *Why does the maternal figure that origination, when the maternal itself must be produced from a larger world of sensuous relations?* To what extent does Merleau-Ponty's insistence on this prior world of flesh offer a way to disjoin the feminine from the controlling figuration of the maternal and offer bodies a way to signify outside the binary trap of mothers and men?

Significantly, for Merleau-Ponty, this fleshly substrate of things cannot be named (and cannot be reduced to any of the names by which it is approached, thus signifying the limits of the indexical function of the name). For Merleau-Ponty, language enters this scene as precisely what can trace and encode the peregrinations of reversible relations, trace and encode substitutions, but what cannot itself reveal that conditioning "flesh" that constitutes the medium in which these relations occur, a medium that would include the flesh of language itself. Indeed, language is secondary to this ontological notion of the "flesh," and Merleau-Ponty will describe it as the second life of this flesh. At the same time, he will claim that if we were to give a full account of the body and its senses, we would see that "all the possibilities of language are given in it."[6]

If language then emerges from and directly reflects these prior movements of bodily life, then it would seem that language is as subject to the charge of solipsism as were these prior relations. And part of what he writes seems to support this point. In a lyrical and unfinished set of notes that constitute the closing paragraphs of his essay, he recalls the circularity of the interrogative in Heidegger: "[I]n opening the horizon of the nameable and of the sayable ... speech acknowledge[s] that it has its place in that horizon ... with one sole gesture [the speaker] closes the circuit of his relation to himself and that of his relations to the others."[7]

The closing of this circuit Irigaray will read as a sign of a pervasive solipsism. As a caricature of his position, she writes, "Speech is not used to communicate, to encounter, but to talk to oneself, to duplicate and reduplicate oneself, to surround, even to inter oneself."[8] This is speech that closes off the addressee, that is not properly allocutory, or that can figure the addressee only on the model of the speaker himself. This presumption of the substitutability of the speaker and the addressed is, for Irigaray, the denial of sexual difference, which she will argue always sets a limit to relations of linguistic substitutability. Of Merleau-Ponty's final remarks, she writes:

> No new speech is possible here. . . . A Word that no longer has an *open* future and consequently shuts out certain enunciatory practices: cries for help, announcements, demands, expressions of gratitude, prophecy, poetry. . . . Necessarily, an other is present in these practices, but not that allocutor for whom I can substitute myself, whom I can anticipate. The circuit is open. Meaning does not function like the circularity of something given and received. It is still in the process of making itself.[9]

This language, then, is not yet ethical, for it cannot yet pose a question the answer to which it does not already possess: "In a certain way, this subject never enters the world. He never emerges from an osmosis that allows him to say to the other, 'Who art Thou?' But also, 'Who am I?' . . . The phenomenology of the flesh that Merleau-Ponty attempts is without question(s)."[10]

But is this right? Does Irigaray's critique not rest on the faulty presumption that to be implicated in the Other or in the world that one seeks to know is to have that Other and that world be nothing more than a narcissistic reflection of oneself? Does Irigaray's own textual implication in Merleau-Ponty's text not refute the very thesis that she explicitly defends? For she finds herself "implicated" there, but she is not, for that reason, the source or origin of that text; it is, rather, the site of her expropriation. One might well conclude that for Merleau-Ponty, as well, to be implicated in the world of flesh of which he is a part is to realize precisely that he cannot disavow such a world without disavowing himself, that he is abandoned to a world that is not his to own. Similarly, if the "Other" is so fundamentally and ontologically foreign, then the ethical relation must be one of sanctimonious apprehension from a distance. On the contrary, if Merleau-Ponty "is" the Other, without the Other being reducible to him, then he meets the Other not in an encounter with the outside, but with a discovery of his own internal impossibility, of the Other who constitutes him internally. To have one's being implicated in the Other is thus to be intertwined from the start, but not for that reason to be reducible to—or exchangeable with—one another. Moreover, to be implicated elsewhere from the start suggests that the subject, as flesh, is primarily an intersubjective being, finding itself as Other, finding its primary sociality in a set of relations that are never fully recoverable or traceable. This view stands in stark contrast both to the Freudian conception of the "ego," understood as the site of a primary narcissism, and to the various forms of atomistic individualism derived from Cartesian and liberal philosophical traditions. Indeed, the flesh, understood to reflect the narcissism of the subject, establishes the limits of that narcissism in a strong way.

Finally, let me draw attention to one dimension of Merleau-Ponty's philosophical writing that seems to me to resist closure and to resist the circularity of solipsism that Irigaray describes. Let us return to the relation between touch and sight. Is there something that underlies or connects these relations? And can it be described at all? Merleau-Ponty writes, "My left hand is always on the verge of touching my right hand touching the things, but I never reach coincidence; the coincidence eclipses at the moment of realization." "[T]he incessant escaping"—as he calls it—"is not a failure ... is not an ontological void ... it is spanned by the total being of my body, and by that of the world."[11] But here, it seems the phenomenological experience of not being able to close this circuit, of being, as it were, in a perpetual relationship of noncoincidence with oneself, is asserted only then to be retracted through the postulation of a body and world that overcomes all such appearances of noncoincidence. Can Merleau-Ponty's own description hold? Or does he give signs that he cannot describe what holds these relations together, that the criss-crossing between touch and sight and language is not always reducible to a continuous and self-referential body?

Remember that he describes this *"chassé-crossé"* as a chiasm and that the rhetorical figure of the chiasm is such that two different relations are asserted that are not altogether commutative. A chiasm or chiasmus is defined by *Webster's* as "an inverted relationship between the syntactic elements of parallel phrases," but in the *OED*, it is specified as "a grammatical figure by which the order of words in one of two parallel clauses is inverted in the other." But note that while there is a formal symmetry in the figure of the chiasm, there is no semantic equivalence between the two phrases symmetrically so paired. For when we say, "When the going gets tough, the tough get going," we actually use two different meanings for "going" and two different meanings for "tough" so that the statements appear to be commutative without, in fact, expressing a relationship of semantic equivalence. What is it that escapes substitutability or equivalence here? I think it is the very capacity of language to mean more and differently than it appears, a certain possibility for semantic excess that exceeds the formal or syntactic appearance of symmetry. For the hand that touches is not identical to the hand that is touched, even if it is the same hand, and this noncoincidence is a function of the temporally noncoincident ontology of the flesh. And the "tough" who get going are not quite the same as the "tough" that adjectivally qualified a certain kind of going. Here, meaning is displaced in the course of the claim, as a kind of metonymic effect of writing itself. And this might be understood as precisely the kind of "exceeding of itself" or "escaping of itself" of language that cannot be quite closed up or closed down by the putative project of solipsism that Irigaray claims governs Merleau-Ponty's text.

In this way, we might ask whether Merleau-Ponty's own writing, a writing that, important in this chapter, did not have closure, remained open-ended, and finally failed to make peace with its burgeoning set of claims, whether this excessive text did not in the end need its editor and its reader—shall we call this its allocutory "Other," its Irigaray— in order to exist for us at all?

After all, it will be this text from which Irigaray cites and derives her own notion of the "two lips" and that she mimes into a feminist usage that Merleau-Ponty could not have intended. Does this not signify a life of the text that exceeds whatever solipsism afflicts its inception and that makes itself available for an Irigarayan appropriation, one in which, in substituting herself for him, she derives a feminist contribution to philosophy that is continuous with and a break from what has come before?

Violence, Nonviolence
Sartre on Fanon

What is immediately strange about Sartre's controversial preface to Fanon's *The Wretched of the Earth* is its mode of address.[1] To whom is this preface written? Sartre imagines his reader as the colonizer or the French citizen who recoils from the thought of violent acts of resistance on the part of the colonized. Minimally, his imagined reader is one who believes that his own notions of humanism and universalism suffice as norms by which to assess the war for independence in Algeria and similar efforts at decolonization. Sartre's address to his audience is direct and caustic: "What does Fanon care whether you read his work or not? It is to his brothers that he denounces our old tricks" (12). At one point, he seems to take his implied readers aside, addressing the preface to them directly:

> Europeans, you must open this book and enter into it. After a few steps in the darkness you will see strangers gathered around a fire; come close, and listen, for they are talking of a destiny they will

mete out to your trading centers and to the hired soldiers who defend them. They will see you, perhaps, but they will be talking among themselves, without even lowering their voices. This indifference strikes home: their fathers, shadowy creatures, *your* creatures, were but dead souls; you it was who allowed them glimpses of light, to you only did they dare to speak, and you did not bother to reply to such zombies. . . . Turn and turn about; in these shadows from whence a new dawn will break, it is you who are the zombies [*les zombies, c'est vous*]. (13)

There are many curious aspects of this mode of address. It may well have been presumptuous of Sartre to address those living under conditions of colonization directly, since it would have put him in a position of pedagogical power over them. He has no information to impart *to them*, no advice, no explanation, and certainly no apology for European colonial dominance and, in particular, French colonial rule in Algeria. So he speaks, as it were, to his white brethren, knowing perhaps that his own name on the preface will attract such readers to this text by Fanon. So Sartre, or rather Sartre's name, is bait for the European reader. But do we understand what "Europe" is in this context, or, for that matter, the "European"? Sartre himself assumes that the European is white and a man. And so two separate zones of masculinity are contoured when he imagines Fanon speaking to his brothers, his colonized brothers, in the text, whereas Sartre speaks to his European brothers, collaborators with the powers of colonization, in one way or another.

We might ask whether these two racially divided fraternities are being built through the modes of direct address that structure this text. Matters are made more complex by the fact that Fanon speaks to many audiences, and sometimes his lines of address interrupt each other. A European, in Sartre's view, will read this text only as a kind of eavesdropping: "Europeans, you must open this book and enter into it. After a few steps in the darkness you will see strangers gathered around a fire; come close, and listen [*approchez, écoutez*]" (13). So Fanon's text is a conversation figured as a conversation *among* colonized men, and Sartre's preface is less a conversation among the colonizers than an exhortation of one to the other, asking the European to read as one would listen to a conversation that is *not* meant for the one, the "you" addressed by Sartre. Just as Sartre's preface is not intended for the colonized population (though we might nonetheless consider it as a kind of display of Sartre's politics for them), so Fanon's text is construed as not addressed to a white, European audience. In effect, Sartre writes: "Come listen to this text that is not meant for you, that is not speaking to you, that cuts you out as its audience, and learn why this text had to be addressed instead to those living in the decolonized state of being, that is, neither fully dead nor fully living. Come and listen to the voices that are no longer petitioning you, no longer seeking inclusion in your world, no longer concerned with whether you hear and understand or not." Sartre petitions his European brothers, presumptively white, to bear up under this rejection and indifference and to come to understand the reasons why they are not the intended audience of Fanon's book. Of course, it is unclear how they could come to learn this lesson or see this truth without becoming its audience and reading the book. But that is the paradox at stake here.

In the course of exhorting them to "listen in" on this book, Sartre is positioning a white audience at a curious distance where it is made at once to suffer peripheral status. The white audience can no longer presume itself to be the intended audience, equivalent to "any" reader, anonymous and implicitly universal. The paradox, as I mentioned, is that the white brethren are asked to read on nonetheless and are even exhorted to read on, though their reading on is to be construed as a listening in, instating their outside status at the moment of their comprehension. This seems another way of saying: "This book is for you; you would do well to read it." The kind of displaced comprehending that Sartre proposes for the white reader is one that deconstitutes the presumptive privilege of the European reader in the act of taking in this new historical constellation. Decentering and even rejection are absorbed, undergone, and a certain undoing of the *presumption* of racial privilege is enacted between the lines, or rather in the nonaddress that is paradoxically delivered through Sartre's preface to the European. The preface thus functions as a strange mode of delivery, handing the white reader the discourse not intended for him and so handing him dislocation and rejection as the condition of possibility for his comprehension. Sartre's writing to the European reader is a way of acting upon that reader, positioning him outside the circle and establishing that peripheral status as an epistemological requirement for understanding the condition of colonization. The European reader undergoes a loss of privilege at the same time that he is asked to submit to an empathetic enactment with the position of the socially excluded and effaced.

So Fanon's text, figured by Sartre as plurivocal and fraternal—that is, as a conversation among a group of men—undoes the notion of Fanon the singular author. Fanon is a budding movement. His writing is the speaking of several men. And when Fanon writes, a conversation takes place; the written page is a meeting, one in which strategy is being planned, and a circle is drawn tight among fellow travelers. Outside of the circle are those who understand that this speaking is indifferent to them. A "you" is being spoken around the fire, but the European no longer counts as part of that "you." He may hear the word "you" only to recognize that he is not included within its purview. If we ask how this exclusion came about for the European, Sartre claims that it follows dialectically from the way that white men suspended the humanity of the fathers of those who have lived under colonialism. The sons saw their fathers humiliated, treated with indifference, and now that very indifference has been taken up and returned to its sender in new form.

Interestingly, it is the humanity of the fathers subjugated under colonialism that is at issue here, and that implies that the dehumanization of others under colonialism follows from the erosion of paternal authority. It is this offense that mandates exclusion from the conversation that composes Fanon's text. This is a choreography of men, some forming inner circles, some cast to the periphery, and it is their manhood, or rather the manhood of their fathers, that is at stake in the direct address. Not to be addressed as a "you" is to be treated as less than a man. And yet, as we will see, the "you" functions in at least two ways in Fanon: as the direct address that establishes human dignity through masculinization and as the direct address that establishes the question of the human beyond the framework of masculinization and feminization alike. In either case, though, the "you" does not merely refer to the one who is addressed, but address itself is the condition of becoming a human, one who is constituted within the scene of address.[2]

If the excluded European asks *why* he is not privy to the conversation, then he must consider the implications of being treated with indifference. The problem to consider is not just that colonizers bear bad attitudes toward the colonized. If the colonized are excluded from the conversation in which humans are not only addressed, but constituted through the address, the very possibility of being constituted as a human is foreclosed. To be excluded from the conversation is the unmaking of the human as such. The fathers of these men were not treated as men, certainly not addressed, directly or otherwise, as men, and so, failing that address, they were never fully constituted as human. If we seek to understand their ontology, these men who were never addressed as men, we find that no fixed determination is possible. The face-to-face address to a "you" has the capacity to confer a certain acknowledgment, to include the other in the potentially reciprocal exchange of speech; without that acknowledgment and that possibility for reciprocal address, no human may emerge. In the place of the human, a spectre takes form, what Sartre refers to as the "zombie," the shadow figure who is never quite human and never quite not. So if we are to tell the prehistory of this complex scene of address within Fanon's *The Wretched of the Earth*, or rather the two scenes of address that separate its traditional preface from the text itself, we would begin, according to Sartre, with the view that the colonizers had no "you" for the colonized, could and would not address them directly, and as a result, withheld a certain ontological determination, one that follows only through recognition as a reciprocal exchange, a mutually constituting set of acts.

The colonizer had no "you" for the colonized, and in Sartre's preface again, but paradoxically, the "you" is reserved exclusively for the colonizer. Who will speak to the colonized? For Fanon, the colonizer is not the "you," or so Sartre tells us, but for Sartre, the colonized is not the "you." So Sartre continues the very tradition of nonaddress that he seeks to indict. Sartre speaks as a spectral double: at once, in the name of the European who shows how deconstituting his own privilege is apparently done, but also in a prescriptive vein, calling upon other Europeans to do the same. When Sartre effectively says " 'You' are not the intended reader of this text," he constitutes the group who ought to undergo the deconstitution of their privilege; in addressing them, however, he does not deconstitute them, but rather constitutes them anew. The problem, of course, is that in addressing them as the privileged, as one privileged speaker to another, he solidifies their privilege, as well. And where before, the colonizers, in withholding address from the colonized, imperiled an ontological determination for them, now, in Sartre's usage, the "you"—directed toward his European counterparts—is being asked to assume responsibility for this colonial condition of destitution. Sartre mobilizes the second person, strikes out with his "you," in order to accuse and demand accountability: "their fathers, shadowy creatures, *your* creatures, were but dead souls; *you* it was who allowed them glimpses of light, to you only did they dare to speak, and you did not bother to reply to such zombies" (13, my emphasis).

In the stark scene of colonial subjugation that Sartre lays out, the colonized did not address each other, but only spoke to *you*, the colonizer. If they could have addressed one another, they would have started to take shape within a legible social ontology; they would have risked existence through this communicative circuit. They dared to speak only to "you"—in other words, you were the exclusive audience for any direct address. You (the colonizer) did not bother to reply, for to reply would have meant to confer a certain human status on the one speaking to you. The mode of address, far from being a simple rhetorical technique, enacts the social constitution of ontology. Or let me put it more starkly: The mode of address enacts the social possibility of a livable existence. Correspondingly, refusing to reply to or address another who speaks, or requiring an asymmetrical form of address according to which the one in power is the exclusive audience for the second person—these are all ways of deconstituting ontology and orchestrating a nonlivable life. This is clearly the paradox of dying while alive, a further permutation of what Orlando Patterson, invoking Hegel in the context of describing slavery, called *social death*.[3] And there, as well as here, this social death touches fathers first, which means it leaves its legacy of shame and rage for the sons. Most importantly, social death is not a static condition, but a perpetually lived contradiction that takes shape as a particularly masculine conundrum. In the context of Algeria and the war for independence, the colonized man is left with a choice that cannot culminate in a livable life: "If he shows fight," Sartre writes, "the soldiers fire and he's a dead man; if he gives in, he degrades himself and he is no longer a man at all; shame and fear will split up his character and make his inmost self fall to pieces" (15).

Of what use is it for the European man to know of this impossible choice, of this historical formation of the life and death struggle within Algerian colonialism? Although Fanon's book is *not* written as a petition to the European liberal to see his complicity with the violence in Algeria, Sartre's preface clearly is. Sartre imagines his interlocutor: "[I]n this case, you will say, let's throw away this book. Why read it if it is not written for us?" (13). Sartre offers two reasons, and they are worth drawing attention to here: The first is that the book gives those for whom it is not intended, the European elite, a chance to understand themselves. The collective subject designated by the "we" is reflected back to themselves in an objective mode through the "scars" (*blessures*) and the "chains" (*fers*) of our victims. What, he asks, have we made of ourselves? In a sense, Fanon's work gives the European man a chance to know himself and so to engage in the pursuit of self-knowledge, based upon an examination of his shared practices, that is proper to the philosophical foundations of human life, as Sartre understands it.

The second reason he gives is that "Fanon is the first since Engels to bring the processes of history [*l'accoucheuse de l'histoire*] into the clear light of day" (apart from Georges Sorel, whose work Sartre considers to be fascist) (14). What is meant by the "processes" of history here? In what sense are they delivering the past, as a midwife would? And through what means are such facilitations brought to light? The process of history is dialectical, but the situation of the colonized is a "portrait"—to use Albert Memmi's term—of a dialectical movement at an impasse. Sartre predicts that decolonization is a historical necessity nonetheless, precisely because the effort to annihilate the other is never fully successful. Capitalism requires the labor power of the colonized. "Because," Sartre writes, the colonizer "can't carry massacre on to genocide, and slavery to animal-like degradation, he loses control, the machine goes into reverse, and a relentless logic leads him on to decolonization" (16).

So we can see at least two further purposes at work in Sartre's preface at this point. He is arguing, on the one hand, that the scars and chains of the colonized here brought to light reflect back the colonizer to himself, and in this they become instrumental to the European task of self-knowledge. On the other hand, he is arguing that the scars and the chains are, as it were, the motors of history, the pivotal moments; as the animating traces of a subjugation just short of death, these scars and chains mobilize an inexorable historical logic that, in turn, culminates in the demise of colonial power. In the first instance, the scars and chains reflect not only the actions of European power, but also the default implications of European liberalism. For while the liberal opposes violence and considers colonial violence to be part of what happens elsewhere, the liberal also endorses a version of the state that marshals violence in the name of preserving that liberalism against a putative barbarism. I want to suggest that the scars and chains are *in this regard* considered instrumental, producing a reflection of the violence of European liberalism, but only as part of the larger reflexive project of self-knowledge, self-critique, and even self-deconstitution on the part of a European elite. In the second instance, the scars and chains are understood as signs of an unfolding historical logic, one that conditions and drives the agency of the colonized as they oppose colonialism by every means possible.

These two ways of considering suffering under colonialism maintain a distance from the humanist point of view that would simply and emphatically oppose such suffering as morally wrong. Sartre openly worries about a liberal humanism that is blind to the political conditions of morally objectionable suffering, since one could oppose the suffering on moral grounds and leave unchanged the political conditions that regenerate it again and again. Suffering under colonialism thus needs to be situated politically. And within such a context, suffering of this kind, although deplorable, or precisely because it is deplorable, constitutes a resource for political movements. The scars and chains figure in at least two ways, *both* as the effects of criminal deeds *and* as the motors of history—a notion to which I will return shortly. At worst, a European liberal can oppose suffering under colonialism without necessarily engaging in a critique of the state formation that outsources its violence to preserve its spuriously humanist self-definition. If there are parallels with our contemporary political situation, especially with the outsourcing of torture, that is not by accident, since the colonial condition is by no means definitively past.

In a new forward to *The Wretched of the Earth*, Homi Bhabha asks explicitly what this tract concerning decolonization has to say to the present circumstance of globalization.[4] He notes that whereas decolonization anticipates the "freedom" of the postcolonial, globalization is preoccupied with the "strategic denationalization of state sovereignty" (xi). And whereas decolonization sought to establish new national territories, globalization confronts a world of transnational connections and circuitry. Rightly, Bhabha rejects the historiography that would posit the succession of colonialism by postcolonialism and then, ultimately, by globalization in the current epoch. In Bhabha's terms, colonialism persists within the postcolonial, and "the colonial shadow falls across the successes of globalization" (xii). Within globalization, dual economies are established that produce profitable circumstances for an economic elite and institute "persistent poverty and malnutrition, caste and racial injustice" (ibid.). This is, of course, the case that has been made concerning neoliberal strategies within globalization, as well. In Bhabha's argument, though, "[t]he critical language of duality—whether colonial or global—is part of the *spatial* imagination that seems to come so naturally to geopolitical thinking of a progressive, postcolonial cast of mind: margin and metropole, center and periphery, the global and the local, the nation and the world" (xiv).

As much as these divisions persist, it may be that Fanon offers us a way to think beyond these polarities and thus takes a certain distance from the instant binarism of Sartre's preface. Bhabha, for instance, sees in Fanon a trenchant critique of these polarities in the name of a future that will introduce a new order of things. Bhabha discerns the critique of these polarities through the specific rhetorical use of the term "Third World" in Fanon. The "third" is the term that will destabilize the polarities of colonization, and it constitutes a placeholder for the future itself. Thus, Bhabha cites Fanon: " 'The Third World must start over a new history of Man' " (xiv).

Fanon's text, in Bhabha's view, creates a way of understanding moments of transition, especially in those political economies and political vocabularies that seek to get beyond the partitions bequeathed by the Cold War. What is important about these moments of transition is their "incubational" status, to use a Gramscian term. Bhabha claims that "'[n]ew' national, international, or global emergences create an unsettling sense of transition" (xvi). He maintains that Fanon, rather than remaining content with the establishment of a new nationalism, conducts a nuanced critique of ethnonationalism. In Bhabha's view, Fanon's contribution consists in supplying a picture of the "global future" as "an ethical and political project—yes, a plan of action as well as a projected aspiration" (ibid.).

Bhabha's reading implies moving beyond the established grounds of a humanism to repose the question of the human as one that must open up a future. We might well wonder whether humanism has had such established grounds, and this seems reasonable to ask. But let me make the point more precisely: if we object to the suffering under colonialism, even decry it, without calling for a basic transformation of the structures of colonialism, then our objection remains at that register of moral principle that can attend only to the deleterious effects of political systems without attempting a broader social transformation of the conditions that generate those effects. This does not mean that we have to retract our objections to suffering, but only that we must exchange that form of humanism for an inquiry that asks: What has happened to the very notion of the human under such conditions? Our objections to suffering then become part of an operation of critique and a way of opening up the human to a different future.

But even if we get this far with the argument, we are still left with the question of violence and what precisely its role is in the making of the human. Bhabha reads Fanon's discussion of insurrectionary violence as "part of a struggle for psycho-affective survival and a search for human agency in the midst of oppression" (xxxvi). Violence holds out the possibility of acting, of agency, and it also rebels against a social death, even as it cannot escape the parameters of violence and potential death. Indeed, under these conditions of colonial subjugation, violence is a wager and a sign that there is an ongoing psychoaffective struggle to be. Sartre, however, is less equivocal, at least in these pages, on the role of violence in the making of the human, even within the horizon of posthumanism. If for Nietzsche the categorical imperative is soaked in blood, then for Sartre, a certain kind of humanism surely is soaked in blood, as well.

In both Sartre's preface and Bhabha's forward there is a question of the human to come. Their writings precede Fanon's text, but come later, and the question they pose before Fanon's text begins to be read is whether there is a future for the human opened up by this text. There is in both prefatory writings a way of thinking about the human beyond humanism, and this is part of what the Sartrean preface tries to do, in the mode and through the example of direct address. When Sartre writes "you," he is trying to bring down one version of man and bring about another. But his performative appellations do not have the force of God's, so something invariably misfires, and we find ourselves in a bind. Is Sartre perhaps posing as a superhuman agent in thinking he can destroy and make man in the image he so desires? Just as the performative force of Sartre's direct address does not straightaway bring about a new man, neither do the scars and chains straightaway bring about the end of colonialism. Finally, though, we have to understand whether for Sartre, violence is generative of a "new man"—and whether, in saying that this is also Fanon's view, Sartre is rightly citing him or making free use of his text for his own purposes.

I will hope to show that it is a specific cultural formation of the human that Sartre traces and applauds here, one that I would call masculinist, yet it seems important to keep in mind that in Fanon, and perhaps in Sartre, as well, there is both a demand for a restitution of masculinism as well as an effort to query who the "you" might be beyond the strictures of gender. Sartre's effort to think the human on the far side of a certain kind of liberal humanism cannot resolve the equivocation at the heart of *homme* as both "man" and "human." But certain possibilities nevertheless emerge from that equivocal designator; interestingly, it is the "you"—the second person—that disrupts its usual signifying circuits.

Sartre clears textual space for the reflexivity of the European man—his perennial first-person task to know himself. But does the colonized have any such reflexivity? Sartre locates the mobilizing wounds of the colonized that produce decolonization as a historical inevitability, as if those wounds did not have to pass through the reflexive subjectivity of the wounded. In this way, he seems to eclipse the reflexivity of the colonized in his preface. This is evident not only in the politesse with which Sartre refuses to address the colonized, reiterating a non-address that he himself diagnoses as the root of their suspended humanity, but in his treatment of counterinsurgent violence as if it were a determined or mechanized reaction and precisely *not* the deliberative or reflective decision of a set of political subjects engaged in a political movement. Indeed, when we ask about the agency of insurgent anticolonial violence, it turns out that the only real agent of violence is that of the colonizer. Sartre says as much when he claims that "at first, it will only be the settler's force" (17; my translation). In arguing this, Sartre seeks to derive the violence of colonial insurrection from the primacy of state violence, casting revolutionary violence as a secondary effect of a primary form of violent oppression. If the colonized respond with violence, their violence is nothing other than a transposition or transmutation of the violence done to them. Fanon's formulation differs slightly from the Sartrean account when Fanon claims, in the first chapter of *Wretched* called "Concerning Violence," that

[t]he violence which has ruled over the ordering of the colonial world, which has ceaselessly drummed the rhythm for the destruction of native social forms and broken up without reserve the systems of reference of the economy, the customs of dress and external life, will be claimed and taken over by the native at the moment when, deciding to embody history in his own person, he surges into forbidden quarters. (40)

The violence travels, passes hands, but can we say that it remains the settler's violence? Does it actually belong to either party, if the violence remains the same as it shifts from the violence imposed by the ruler to the violence wielded by the colonized? It would seem to be fundamentally transferable. But this is not the Sartrean view. Indeed, his view makes the colonizer into the primary subject of violence. And this claim seems to contradict his other claim, namely, that under these conditions, violence can be understood to bring the human into being. If we subscribe to his first thesis, we are left with the conclusion, surely faulty, that colonization is a precondition for humanization, something that civilizational justifications for colonization have always maintained and a view that, we would have to surmise, Sartre wanted vehemently to oppose.

Sartre makes several efforts to account for violent resistance on the part of the colonized. He takes on the charge leveled by colonialists that there are simply base or animal instincts at work in these apparently precivilizational peoples. Sartre asks: "What instincts does he mean? The instincts that urge slaves to massacre their master? Can he not here recognize his own cruelty turned against himself?" (16). Anticipating his claim that "the only violence is the settler's," he remarks here that the colonizer finds in the violence of the colonized only his own violence. The colonized are said to have "absorbed" the settler's cruelty through every pore. And though the colonized are said to take in and take on the violence by which they are oppressed, as if through the inexorable force of transitivity, the colonized are also said to become who they are by the "deep-seated refusal of that which others have made of [them]" (17).

Here, Sartre seems to subscribe to a theory of psychological absorption or mimeticism that would simply transfer the violence of the colonizer onto and into the violence of the colonized. In his view, the colonized absorb and recreate the violence done to them, but they also refuse to become what the colonized have made of them (17). If this is a contradiction, it is one in which the colonized are forced to live. Just as, earlier, we remarked upon the impossible choice: "If he shows fight . . . he's a dead man; if he gives in, he degrades himself." He is made violent by the violence done to him, but this violence puts his own life at risk; if he fails to become violent, he remains its victim, and "shame and fear will split up his character and make his inmost self fall to pieces" (15). Shame, because he could not or would not assume violence to counter violence, and fear, since he knows how precarious and extinguishable his life finally is under violently imposed colonial rule.

The problem of violence, then, seems to appear here in what Bhabha calls "psycho-affective survival," a self imperiled by shame and fear, one that is internally split up and at risk of falling into pieces. The question is whether anything can stop this fatal splintering of the self and why violence appears as the route toward selfhood, agency, and even life. Note that this self is distinct from the one who simply absorbs or uncritically mimes and returns the violence done against him. There is, here, a passage through a decimated self that has to be navigated, and violence appears as one route out. Is it the only route? And did Fanon think so?

In order to answer this, we have first to understand what happens to violence when it is taken up or taken on by the colonized in the name of an insurgent resistance. It is only "at first" that violence is the settler's, and then, later, it is made into their own. Is the violence that the colonized make into their own different from the violence imposed upon them by the settler's? When Sartre endeavors to explain this secondary violence, the one derived from the colonizing settler, he remarks that it is "thrown back upon us as when our reflection comes forward to meet us when we go toward a mirror" (17). This description suggests that the insurgent violence is nothing but the reflection of the colonizer's violence, as if a symmetry exists between them, and the second follows only as the dialectical reflection of the first. But this cannot be fully true. Since the colonizer "no longer remembers clearly that he was once a man; he takes himself to be a horsewhip or

a gun" (16), violence is precisely the means through which the colonized become men. Later, he remarks that the "European has only been
able to become a man through creating slaves and monsters" (26). So
it would appear that Sartre maintains at least two different conceptions of the human here. The colonizer forgets that he is a man when
he becomes violent, but the particular sort of man that he becomes is
dependent on this violence. As I mentioned earlier, Sartre uses the term
homme for *humain* here, and the equivocation runs deep throughout the
argument. But it would seem that the colonizer who has forgotten that
he is a "man" becomes a horsewhip or a gun by virtue of being crazed
with the fear of losing his absolute power. That colonizer seeks to at-
tack precisely those men he does not regard as men and who, by virtue of this violent encounter, run the risk of being a horsewhip or a
gun as well.

So many men seem to be forgotten in this scene. Who is this forgotten man? And who is the man to come? The colonized is said to
become a "man" through violence, but we know that the violence that
the colonized takes on is at first the settler's violence. But does the
colonized separate from the settler's violence, and does this very separation serve as a condition of the "becoming human" of the colonized?
Sartre is clear that the "hidden anger" that various forms of humanism condemn is actually "the last refuge of their humanity" (18). In
that anger Sartre reads both the effect of colonial legacy as well as the
refusal of that legacy, a knot, a contradiction, that produces a finally
unlivable bind and then a demand for total change. Violence becomes
a clear alternative when a life of continuing famine and oppression
seems far worse than death (20). At this point, Sartre writes, "there is
only one duty to be done, one end to achieve: to thrust out colonialism by *every* means in their power" (21). Sartre's portrayal of insurgent
violence is meant to provide insight into the person who lives under
such oppression. As such, it serves as a reconstruction of an induced
psychological state. It also reads as a fully instrumental rationaliza-
tion for violence and thus as a normative claim. Indeed, the violent

acts by which decolonization is achieved are also those by which man "recreates himself" (ibid.). Sartre is describing a psychopolitical reality, but he is also offering, we might say, a new humanism to confound the old, one that requires, under these social conditions, violence to materialize. He writes, "no gentleness can efface the marks of violence, only violence itself can destroy them" (ibid.).[5] Of course, we have to ask whether violence itself, said to efface the marks of violence, does not simply make more such marks, leaving new legacies of violence in its wake.

Moreover, weren't those very scars and chains necessary to motor the revolution? The scars and chains served a double purpose: first, they reflected back to the European the consequences of his failed humanism, his exported colonial domination; second, they were said to animate the inexorable logic of decolonization in history and are now precisely what stand to be "effaced" through the acts of violence that effect that decolonization. These scars and chains serve as mirrors for the European, serve as historical motors for the colonized, and are finally negated, if not fully transformed, through the act of self-creation. The existential *dicta* to know and to create oneself thus makes its appearance toward the end of Sartre's provocative preface when he claims that the violent acts of the colonized finally establish him as the existential subject par excellence: "When his rage boils over, he rediscovers his lost innocence and he comes to know himself in that he himself creates his self" (21). Of course, this self-making is a curious one, since the violence seems to be induced by a historically inevitable dialectical development, but this form of determinism is not yet reconciled with the theory of self-constitution in Sartre, and the tension between the two positions turns out to bear significant implications.

Sartre began his preface with an allocation of pronouns according to a strict division of labor. Fanon will speak to the colonized; Sartre will speak to the European, especially the liberal man in France who understands himself to be morally and politically at a distance from the events in Algeria and the French colonies. Sartre will not speak to the colonized, and we presume that this is so because he does not want to occupy a morally didactic position. He suggests that the Europeans listen in and that they be made to suffer their peripheral status to the conversation at hand. And yet Sartre will characterize through a psychological portrait the violence of the colonized and then claim that the man who engages in violent acts of overthrow fulfills his own existential Marxism. In deconstituting the social conditions of dehumanization, the colonized effects his own decolonization and through this double-negation makes himself a man: "[T]his new man," Sartre writes, "begins his life as a man at the end of it; he considers himself as a potential corpse" (23). To say that the man is potentially dead is to say that he lives this potentiality in the present, so that death is hardly risked; it functions as an epistemic certainty, if not a defining feature of his existence. Bhabha refers to this as a "life-in-death." Finally to die is thus to realize what has already been mandated as true or necessary. And yet to die in the service of deconstituting these conditions of social death is done precisely in the name of future life and future men.

It is in this preface, you will remember, that Sartre debunks Camus's earlier position on nonviolence.[6] The believers in nonviolence, he quips, say that they are "neither executioners nor victims" (25). But Sartre refuses the effort to sidestep this binary alternative, claiming instead that nonviolence and passivity are tantamount to complicity, and, entering into a direct address, remarks that "your passivity serves only to place you in the ranks of the oppressors" (ibid.). What is required is a deconstitution of the notion of man, especially if to be a man, as Sartre claims, is to be an accomplice to colonialism. Only through the deconstitution of this version of being a man can the history of the human unfold. We are not given much of an idea of what the final unfolding of the human will look like, but Sartre offers a brief remark toward the end of the essay where he imagines a history of humankind that culminates in a future state of becoming "full-grown." When human kind reaches this state, he claims, "it will not define itself as the sum total of the world's inhabitants, but as the infinite unity of their mutual needs" (27).

Here, at the end of a piece that is widely regarded as an encomium to violence, Sartre takes another turn, manifesting perhaps at this juncture the fundamental ambivalence of his views on violence, one that has been ably demonstrated in Ronald Santoni's *Sartre on Violence: Curiously Ambivalent.*[7] Obviously, this vision of the infinite unity of mutual needs that might exist among the world's inhabitants is one in which physical need and vulnerability would become matters for mutual recognition and regard. If we consider what Fanon claims about violence, we can see there as well a certain understanding that violence has its place in the overcoming of colonialism, but also a recognition that it brings with it a nihilism, a corrosive spirit of absolute negation. If he argues that there can be no other way under such conditions of oppression, he argues as well that such conditions of oppression must be fully overcome in order for violence no longer to pervade social life. What is remarkable about Fanon's view, perhaps put more strongly than Sartre is willing to replicate, is that the body itself becomes historical precisely through an embodiment of social conditions. The wrecked and muted body is not merely an example of the condition of colonial rule; it is its instrument and effect, and moreover, colonial rule *is not* without such instruments and effects. The destitution of the body is not only an effect of colonialism, where colonialism is understood as something prior, something separate, a "condition" both analytically and historically separate from the body at issue. On the contrary, *the body is the animated, or rather deanimated life of that historical condition, that without which colonization itself cannot exist.* Colonization is the deadening of sense, the establishment of the body in social death, as one that lives and breathes its potentiality as death, and so working and reproducing its force at the somatic and affective level.

It would seem, then, that any effort to reconstruct the human after humanism, that is, after humanism's complicity with colonialism, would have to include an understanding of humans as those who may suffer death in advance of the cessation of bodily function, who suffer it at the heart of life itself. If humans are those kinds of beings who depend on social conditions to breathe and move and live, then it is precisely at the psychophysical level that the human is being redefined in Fanon. This is a psyche that is "crushed with inessentiality" and a body that is restricted in its fundamental mobility. There are places it may not go, first-person utterances it may not inhabit and compose, ways in which it cannot know or sustain itself as an "I." It has not come to know itself as the "you" addressed by the other, and so when it addresses itself, it misses its mark, vacillating between a certitude of its nonexistence and an inflated notion of its future power.

If there is a cult of masculinism that emerges from this situation, perhaps it is explained by Fanon's description of the fantasy of muscular power. Showing his own alliances with a European educated class and with a civilizational project, Fanon proceeds to offer his own portrait of his psychological circumstances. He describes first the facts of spatial restriction: "the indigenous person" is hemmed in, learns that there are places he cannot go, becomes defined by this limitation on spatial motility. Consequently, the idea of himself that compensates for this restriction takes on hyperbolic forms: "This is why the dreams of the native [indigène] are always of muscular prowess; his dreams are of action and aggression. I dream I am jumping, swimming, running, climbing; I dream I burst out laughing, that I span a river in one stride, or that I am followed by a flood of motorcars which never catch up with me" (52).

Fanon regards this hypermuscularity, this superhuman capacity for action, to be compensatory, impossible, fantasmatic, but fully understandable under such conditions. When he claims that the oppressed dream of becoming the persecutor, he is giving us a psychosocial description of the fantasies that take hold under such conditions. He is not necessarily arguing for them, although he will also oppose both nonviolence and compromise as political options during the war for independence in 1961. His argument is strategic: if the decolonized decide upon violence, it is only because they are already in the midst of violence. Violence was not only done in the past, but violence is what continues to happen to them and so forms the horizon of political life. Thus, it is a matter of seizing violence and giving it a new turn. He writes: "Now the problem is to lay hold of this violence which is changing direction" (58). Violence here is not defended as a way of life, and certainly not as a way of imagining the normative goal of a social movement. It is an instrumentality in the service of invention.

Of course, there is a question of whether violence as a pure instrument can remain as such or whether it comes to define, haunt, and afflict the polity that instates itself through violent means. Neither Sartre nor Fanon asks this question. Whether the aspiration is either to create man anew, or to produce a community defined as an infinite unity of mutual needs, or to achieve decolonization, then we have to ask whether violence continues to play a role in what it means to create oneself, what it means to produce such a community, what it means to achieve and sustain decolonization as a goal. It seems clear that violence drops out of the picture when we imagine a community defined as an infinite unity of mutual needs. And violence would not necessarily have a role to play once an unequivocal decolonization is achieved—if that, indeed, proves possible. Where the role of violence is most difficult to understand is in the model of self-creation. It might be easy enough to say that only under the conditions of colonization does violence emerge as a key means through which man makes himself and that without colonization, self-making is no longer achieved through violent means. This position would distinguish itself from one that models self-making on violent negation, that is, the position that claims that all self-making requires violence as a matter of course. Fanon is clear at the end of *The Wretched of the Earth* that the task of decolonization is to create or invent "a new man," one that will not constitute a simple, faithful reflection of European man.

Can we think self-invention in Fanon outside the concept of violence? And if we cannot, is that because violence is necessitated under

192 Violence, Nonviolence

conditions of colonization, the context that limits what he himself can imagine in 1961? Does he, at the end of his book, leave open the possibility of a new kind of self-making yet to be imagined? Can he not supply it precisely because he is not yet historically there, in the place where it can be imagined?

What seems clear is that to be colonized is to be humiliated as a man and that this castration is unendurable. It is the wife of the colonized who is raped or disregarded, and this is for Fanon an offence to the man, the husband, more profoundly than to the woman herself. Rey Chow and others have examined the pervasive masculinism in Fanon's work, and I do not want to belabor it here.[8] But I do want to make two points that lead us toward another way of thinking. First, it strikes me that Fanon understands masculine violent fantasy as compensatory, and this suggests that he understands the fantasmatic dimension of a hypermasculinism. As such, it does not serve as a moral ideal toward which the decolonized should strive. Rather, it serves as a motivational component in the struggle toward decolonization. The distinction is important, since it would follow that under conditions of decolonization, hypermasculinity as a fantasmatic ideal would lose its force as a compensatory motivation for conduct and as a fantasmatic model for self-making. A gendered man would have to cross a river like any other mortal: decolonization does not promise godlike powers, and if it does, necessarily fails to make good on its word.

Although Sartre restrictively makes use of the "you" to constitute and deconstitute his European reader and to divide two different fraternities, the colonizers and the colonized, Fanon offers another version of direct address that moves beyond this rigid binary and that holds out the possibility of thinking the human apart from "man." When, for instance, Fanon prays to his body at the end of *Black Skin, White Masks*, "O my body, make of me always a man who questions!" he calls for a kind of openness that is at once bodily and conscious. He addresses himself and seeks to reconstitute himself through a direct address to his own body. As if countering the psychoaffective dying in life that pervades the lived experience of the colonized, Fanon seeks to prompt the body into an open-ended inquiry. In the line directly preceding, he posits a new collectivity: "I want the world to recognize, with me, the open door of every consciousness [la dimension ouverte de toute conscience]."[9] He asks for recognition of neither his national identity nor his gender, but rather a collective act of recognition that would accord every consciousness its status as something infinitely open. And though he could not have anticipated what that universalizable recognition would mean for gender relations, it is nonetheless there as an incipient and unintended implication of his own words, words that perhaps carry more radical vision than he himself could do nearly a decade later, when he wrote *The Wretched of the Earth*. "O my body"—this cry enacts a certain reflexivity, an address *to oneself* precisely as a body *not* crushed by its inessentiality, but conditioning a certain permanent and open question. This body, beseeched through address, is posited as an opening toward the world and toward a radically egalitarian collectivity. There is no God to whom he prays, but a body, one characterized precisely by what it does not yet know. This moment is doubtless repeated at the end of *The Wretched of the Earth*, despite the profound differences between these two texts. At the end of *Wretched*, Fanon does not know what new version of man will be invented once decolonization takes place. There is an openness toward the future that is far from the omniscient claim; indeed, it is emphatically unknowing and nonprescriptive about what will come.

Perhaps I seize upon this call to his own body to open again to a world, and more radically, to join with others in recognizing the opening of every consciousness precisely because it posits an alternative to the hyperresolute masculinism of anticolonial violence. Of course, *Black Skin, White Masks* was written nine years prior to *The Wretched of the Earth*, but perhaps they can be read together to consider in what this new invention of man, or, indeed, this notion of the human might consist. After all, the call to arms and the critique of pacifism and compromise demand that for the moment, the police, or the white Algerian, or the government official *not* be understood as one whose consciousness is an "open dimension." Indeed, violence against the other *closes* that consciousness, since according to the logic of violence, the "open dimension" of my own consciousness is possible only through closing that dimension in another. According to the argument of *Wretched*, if I am living as the colonized, then to open the door of my own consciousness is possible only through the closing of the door of the other's. It is a life-or-death struggle. At the moment in which I do violence to an other—one who oppresses me, or who represents that oppression, or who is complicitous with that oppression—then I make room not only for my own self-invention, but for a new notion of the human that will not be based on racial or colonial oppression and violence.

At the end of *Black Skin, White Masks*, Fanon addresses himself. This mode of address is not considered in the Sartrean preface, but it remains, perhaps, the most insurrectionary of his speech acts, allegorizing the emergent self-constituting powers of the colonized, unconditioned by any historical or causal necessity. There he writes that only by recapturing and scrutinizing the self can the ideal conditions for a human world come to exist. "Why not," he asks, "the quite simple attempt to touch the other, to feel the other, to explain the other to myself?" (231). This sentence is cast in question form, and it seems to be that self-scrutiny implies this interrogatory relation to the other as a matter of course. He makes this explicit in the next line, when he writes: "Was my freedom not given to me then in order to build the world of the *You*?" (232). We do not know at this moment whether the "you" is the colonized or the colonizer, whether it is also a reaching, a relationality, that constitutes the intentional enthrallment of the "I" as it finds itself outside of itself, enmeshed in the world of others. Self-scrutiny is not merely an inward turn, but a mode of address: *O you, o my body.* This is an appeal as much to his own corporeal life, the restoration of the body as the ground of agency, as it is to the other; it is an address, indeed, a touch, facilitated by the body, one that, for complex reasons, commits itself to regarding each and every consciousness as an open dimension. If the body opens him toward a "you," it opens him in such a way that the other, through bodily means, becomes capable of addressing a "you," as well. Implicit to both modes of address is the understanding of the body, through its touch, securing the open address not just of this tactile other, but of every other body. In this sense, a recorporealization of humanism seems to take hold here that posits an alternative to violence, or, paradoxically, the idea of the unfolded human toward which it strives (and that it must refute in order to realize in the end). Over and against the view that there can be no self-creation without violence, Fanon here exemplifies the philosophical truth that there can be no invention of oneself without the "you" and that the "self" is constituted precisely in a mode of address that avows its constitutive sociality.

When Sartre writes of *Wretched*, "What does Fanon care whether you read his work or not? It is to his brothers that he denounces our old tricks," he seems to be telling us that we may *not* read *Wretched* in light of the "you" that forms the ultimate address *in Black Skin, White Masks*. It is true that in the conclusion to *Wretched*, Fanon addresses "my comrades" and "my brothers." The "you" that closes the earlier work is now specified and restricted, but note that even in *Wretched*, he does *not* call on them to return to ethnic or national identity; no, he calls on them to create a new version of man and so to inaugurate a universality that has never yet been established on this, admittedly wretched, earth. Indeed, what form this universal human may take is unknown, remains a question, and so the opening of the earlier work—the opening toward the "you" facilitated through the body—is finally echoed in the opening that closed the later one. Even in *Wretched*, there is this holding out, finally, for invention, for the new, for an opening that may depend upon a prior violence, but that also presupposes its resolution.

Fanon's address to the body to open and to question, to join in a struggle to recognize the openness of every other embodied consciousness—this struggle toward a new universality—begins, perhaps, precisely when decolonization ends. This would mean that philosophically, *Black Skin, White Masks* would have to follow *The Wretched of the Earth*. The effort to "touch" the "you" in *Black Skin, White Masks* would appear to be very different from the contact that constitutes violent negation. When Sartre refers to the "the infinite unity" of the "mutual needs" of all inhabitants of this earth, he does *not* appeal to everyone's capacity for violence, but rather to the reciprocal requirements that human embodiment implies: food, shelter, protection of life and liberty, means of recognition, and conditions for work and political participation without which no human can emerge or be sustained. The human, in this sense, is both contingent and aspirational, dependent and not yet accomplished or realized.

I am reminded at this moment of that most extraordinary remark that Sartre makes in the 1975 interview with Michel Contat entitled "Self-Portrait at Seventy," where he refers to the prospect of "subjective life" being "offered up" and "given."[10] In the preface to Fanon's *Wretched*, Sartre cannot address the colonized, does not understand it as his place. And yet without such an address, how is a new politics of the human possible? He seems to know in this late interview that the future of the human is instituted through a certain mode of address that reorganizes gender, recalling Fanon, his address to himself and to the "you."

> We yield our bodies to everyone, even beyond the realm of sexual relations: by looking, by touching. You yield your body to me, I yield mine to you: we exist for the other, as body. But we do not exist in the same way as consciousness, as ideas, even though ideas are modifications of the body.
>
> If we truly wished to exist for the other, to exist as body, as body that can continually be laid bare—even if this never actually happens—our ideas would appear to others as coming from the body. Words are formed by a tongue in the mouth. All ideas

would appear in this way, even the most vague, the most fleeting, the least tangible. There would no longer be the hiddenness, the secrecy in certain centuries that was identified with the honor of men and women, and which seems very foolish to me.[11]

Although Sartre holds out for an impossible transparency, for him, such an impossible ideal maintains the ideality and infinite potentiality of desire itself. Of course, "the honor of men and women" holds them in distinct relations, articulates and maintains that difference, but it does more. If emasculation is the sign of dehumanization, then the masculine is the presumptive norm of humanization. That differential norm can only dehumanize in turn, so if, in these strange final confessions, Fanon and Sartre both concede that there is a touch and form of yielding that establishes a relation to a "you," then it would seem that in the place of a struggle over which masculine community will finally prevail, we find a pronoun that is open-ended precisely on the question of gender. It was Arendt who suggested that the question "Who are you?" lies at the basis of participatory democracy.[12] On this basis, the Italian feminist philosopher Adriana Cavarero calls for a rehabilitation of the "you" at the core of politics.[13]

The "you" may well take the place of "man" in the quest for a human beyond the constituted horizon of humanism. If there is a relation between this "you" whom I seek to know, whose gender cannot be determined, whose nationality cannot be presumed, and who compels me to relinquish violence, then this mode of address articulates a wish not just for a nonviolent future for the human, but for a new conception of the human where some manner of touch other than violence is the precondition of that making.

INTRODUCTION

1. Although most of these essays remain in their original form, small editorial changes were made to establish consistency and to correct any former errors.

2. Friedrich Nietzsche, *On the Genealogy of Morals*, trans. Walter Kaufmann and R. J. Hollingdale, in *On the Genealogy of Morals and Ecce Homo*, ed. Walter Kaufmann, (New York: Vintage, 1967), 15.

3. Michel Foucault, "The Politics of Discourse," in *The Foucault Effect: Studies in Governmentality*, ed. Graham Burchell, Colin Gordon, and Peter Miller, (Chicago: University of Chicago Press, 1991), 70–72.

4. See Judith Butler, "The 'I' and the 'You,'" in *Giving an Account of Oneself* (New York: Fordham University Press, 2005), 65–82.

5. After the discovery of thousands of infants and children suffering from sensory deprivation and general neglect in Romanian orphanages in 1989, the year the Ceausescu regime fell, a number of studies sought to link sensory deprivation with developmental and cognitive difficulties in children. Lack of touch and containment impedes development on many different levels, including primary responsiveness. This line of thought can be traced to John Bowlby and Renee Spitz's work on abandoned and neglected children in the early years of psychoanalytic attachment theory in the late 1940s, but these views have taken different form in more recent studies. See Kathleen McCartney and Deborah Phillips, eds., *Blackwell Handbook of Early Child Development* (Malden, MA: Blackwell, 2006), and Deborah A. Frank, et al., "Infants and Young Children in Orphanages:

One View from Pediatrics and Child Psychiatry," *Pediatrics* 97, no. 4 (April 1996): 569–78.

6. Levinas would say that that prior susceptibility is already the ethical. See Emmanuel Levinas, "Sensibility and Proximity," in *Otherwise Than Being, or Beyond Essence,* trans. Alphonso Lingis (Pittsburgh: Duquesne University Press, 1998), 61–98.

7. Denise Riley, "Malediction," in *Impersonal Passion: Language as Affect* (Durham: Duke University Press, 2005), 9–28. See also Riley, "Self-Description's Linguistic Affect," in *Words of Selves: Identification, Solidarity, Irony* (Palo Alto: Stanford University Press, 2000), 22–55.

8. Louis Althusser, "Ideology and Ideological State Apparatuses (Notes Toward an Investigation)," in *Lenin and Philosophy and Other Essays,* trans. Ben Brewster (New York: Monthly Review Press), 1971.

9. Denise Riley, *Am I That Name? Feminism and the Category of Women in History,* (Minneapolis: University of Minnesota Press, 1988).

10. Jean Laplanche, "Implantation, Intromission," in Essays on Otherness, trans. John Fletcher (London: Routledge, 1999), 133–37.

11. For an important set of reflections on philosophy and its ambivalent relation to the body and touch, in particular, see Jacques Derrida, *On Touching— Jean-Luc Nancy,* trans. Christine Irizarry (Palo Alto: Stanford University Press, 2005), 36–65; and Jean-Luc Nancy, *Corpus,* trans. Richard A. Rand, (New York: Fordham University Press, 2008). In both texts, "sense" and "sensation" are not givens that stay the same regardless of context, but are always not what they are, reflexive, intentional, and opened upon other surfaces and sensations and relations, including infinite ones. Nancy's work is most interesting to read as linking Merleau-Ponty's late reflections on touch with the work of Jacques Derrida.

"HOW CAN I DENY THAT THESE HANDS AND THIS BODY ARE MINE?"

This essay was first presented as an invited lecture at the American Philosophical Association Meetings in December 1997, in Philadelphia. It was represented in revised version for the "Culture and Materiality" conference at U.C. Davis in April, 1998 and subsequently was revised for publication in *Qui Parle.*

1. Excellent work reconsidering the relationship of language and materiality in sexual difference has been undertaken by Charles Shephardson, Debra Keates, and Katherine Rudolph.

2. Interestingly, and not without reason, suspended and inscrutable limbs reemerge in de Man's essay "Phenomenality and Materiality in Kant" in ways that suggest a metonymic relation to the problem that Descartes poses. For de Man, the body within the *Third Critique* is understood, if we can use that word, as prior to figuration and cognition. In Descartes, it emerges as a particular kind of figure, one that suspends the ontological status of the term and thus raises the question of any absolute separability between materiality and figuration, a distinction that de Man on some occasions tries to make as absolutely as possible.

3. "Il me fallait entreprendre serieusement une fois en ma vie de me défaire de toutes les opinions que j'avais reçues . . . me défaire de toutes les opinions." The text was originally published in Latin in 1641 in France, although Descartes was living in Holland at the time. Descartes apparently had reasons to fear the Dutch ministers reading the text, and so he had a friend of his oversee its publication in France. It did, however, appear the following year, 1642, in Amsterdam, and the second edition includes the objections and replies. This second edition is usually referred to as the Adam and Tannery version, and it was the basis for the French translations. One of those took place that same year by the Duc de Luynes, and Descartes approved the translation, which is to say that he subjected it to various corrections and revisions. It appeared in revised form in 1647. Hence, we can to some degree think of the French text as one that Descartes approved and, in some instances, wrote, but nevertheless one to which he was willing to attach a signature. Almost every English version of Descartes will be a translation of the second version of the *Meditations*. There were two French translations offered to Descartes for approval, one by the Duc de Luynes and another by Clerselier; he chose the one by the Duc de Luynes for the *Meditations* themselves and the "objections and replies" translation by Clerselier.

In 1661, Clerselier republished his translation, making corrections and abandoning the translation by the Duc de Luynes that Descartes had approved. Many scholarly editions take this to be a more exact and literal translation and have used it as the primary text. Some of them complained that the Duc de Luynes's version was too liberal of a translation, lacking Descartes's exactitude. And they have made excuses for why Descartes might have accepted the translation—politesse, politics, and the like.

The French that I follow here is that provided by the Duc de Luynes. The English is from René Descartes, *Meditations on First Philosophy*, in *The Philosophical Works of Descartes*, trans. Elizabeth Haldane and G. R. T. Ross, vol. 1

(Cambridge: Cambridge University Press, 1973), 144–45. The French is from René Descartes, *Méditations métaphysiques*, ed. Florence Khodoss (Paris: Presses Universitaires de France, 1996), 26.

4. Ibid, 144/26.

5. Ibid., 145/27.

6. Ibid.

7. Ibid., 152/42. In the French, he refers to what is "feintes et inventée par l'imagination," and this notion of "invented" is translated from the Latin: *effingo*. Knowledge of oneself does not depend on what is feigned or invented, but the Latin term Descartes uses for the latter, *effingo*, casts doubt on the very denial that he performs.

8. Ibid. "Je feindrais en effet, si j'imaginais être quelque chose, puisque imaginer n'est autre chose que contempler la figure ou l'image d'une chose corporelle."

9. Descartes writes: "He has at least left within my power . . . firmly to adhere to the resolution never to give judgment on matters whose truth is not clearly known to me; for although I notice a certain weakness in my nature in that I cannot continually concentrate my mind on one single thought [*je ne puis pas attacher continuellement mon esprit à une même pensée*], I cannot continually attach my spirit to the same thought, I can yet, by attentive and frequent meditation, impress [*imprimer*] it so forcibly on my memory that I shall never fail to recollect it whenever I have need of it, and thus acquire the habit of never going astray." Ibid., 178/000.

10. This view corresponds to Lacan's view of the mirror stage as what permits a specular version of the body on the condition of distortion.

11. For a discussion of dismemberment and the limits of figuration, see Paul de Man, "Materiality and Phenomenality in Kant" in *Aesthetic Ideology*, ed. Andrzej Warminski (Minneapolis: University of Minnesota Press, 1997).

12. One might usefully consult Walter Benjamin on the status of allegory for precisely such an approach to the figure.

13. See Jonathan Goldberg, *Writing Matter: From the Hands of the English Renaissance* (Stanford: Stanford University Press, 1990).

MERLEAU-PONTY AND THE TOUCH
OF MALEBRANCHE

1. Maurice Merleau-Ponty, *L'union de l'âme et du corps chez Malebranche, Biran et Bergson*, ed. Jean Deprun (Paris: Vrin, 2002). All citations from this text are

my own translations, although an English version, without the appendix, now exists under the title *The Incarnate Subject: Malebranche, Biran, and Bergson on the Union of Body and Soul*, ed. Andrew J. Bjelland, Jr. and Patrick Burke, trans. Paul B. Milan (Amherst, NY: Humanity Books, 2001).

2. Nicolas Malebranche, "Elucidation Eleven," in *The Search after Truth*, ed. and trans. Thomas M. Lennon and Paul J. Olscamp (Cambridge: Cambridge University Press, 1997), 633–38; see also books one and two, 76–90.

3. See Craig Walton's "Translator's Introduction" to the *Treatise on Ethics (1684)* (Boston: Kluwer, 1993) for a discussion of Malebranche's opposition to neo-Aristotelian accounts of the causal power of beings. For Malebranche, all created things are caused by the divine order and exercise power only in a derivative sense. This is the meaning of his "occasionalism."

4. See Nicolas Malebranche, *Treatise on Nature and Grace*, trans. Patrick Riley (New York: Oxford University Press, 1992), 51–55, 169–94.

5. Jean Deprun explains in his introduction that he consulted the student notebooks from the two versions of this course that Merleau-Ponty gave in the same year and chose between divergent accounts on the basis of which formulation seemed most clear and explicit. He describes his experience as an editor of this volume as "facile," arguing that editorial decisions in no way altered the substantive views of Merleau-Ponty. Although Jacques Taminiaux in his preface to the English version remarks that these are obligatory courses and maintain a tangential relationship to Merleau-Ponty's own explicit philosophical views, I differ with this conclusion because the preoccupation with touch, with alterity, and with an order of intelligibility disclosed through sentience seems crucial to Merleau-Ponty's developing account of bodily experience and its relation to knowledge.

6. Maurice Merleau-Ponty, "Partout et nulle part," in *Signes* (Paris: Gallimard, 1960); Merleau-Ponty, "Everywhere and Nowhere," in *Signs*, trans. Richard C. McCleary (Evanston: Northwestern University Press, 1964). Originally published as an introduction to Maurice Merleau-Ponty, *Les philosophes célèbres* (Paris: Lucien Mazenot, 1956).

7. Ibid., 177/140.

8. Ibid., 178–79/142.

9. Ibid., 181/143–44.

10. Ibid., 183/145.

11. Merleau-Ponty, *L'union de l'âme et du corp*, 24; Merleau-Ponty, *The Incarnate Subject*, 43, translation modified. The sentence is quoted from Malebranche's *Méditations chrétiennes et métaphysiques* and originally reads: "Il est nécessaire que je ne me sente qu'en moi-même, lorsqu'on me touche."

12. Ibid., 18/38.

13. Ibid., 36/53.

14. Ibid., 19/39.

15. Quoted in ibid., 18/38.

16. Ibid., 21/40.

17. Ibid.

18. Ibid., 22/40–41.

19. Malebranche, *The Search after Truth*, 233.

20. Maurice Merleau-Ponty, *Le visible et l'invisible: Suivi de notes de travail*, ed. Claude Lefort (Paris: Gallimard, 1964), 140; Merleau-Ponty, *The Visible and the Invisible: Followed by Working Notes*, ed. Claude Lefort, trans. Alphonso Lingis (Evanston: Northwestern University Press, 1968), 185.

21. Ibid., 146/191–92.

22. Ibid., 147–48/194.

23. Merleau-Ponty, *L'union de l'âme et du corps*, 22; The *Incarnate Subject*, 41.

24. Ibid., 22–23/41.

25. Ibid., 23/41.

26. Ibid., 31/50.

27. Ibid., 31/50.

28. Ibid., 31/50.

29. Ibid., 33/51.

30. Quoted in ibid., 34/54.

31. This appendix is not included in the English translation I've cited.

32. Merleau-Ponty, *L'union de l'âme et du corps*, 116.

33. Ibid., 117.

34. Ibid., 118.

35. Ibid.

THE DESIRE TO LIVE: SPINOZA'S *ETHICS* UNDER PRESSURE

1. Benedict de Spinoza, *A Spinoza Reader: The "Ethics" and Other Works*, ed. and trans. Edwin Curley (Princeton: Princeton University Press, 1994), IIIP6, 159. All further citations to this text will be in the text and include a reference to Spinoza's text as it is usually cited, followed by the page number of the Curley translation.

2. Gilles Deleuze, *Expressionism in Philosophy: Spinoza*, trans. Martin Joughin (New York: Zone Books, 1990).

3. Sigmund Freud, *Civilization and Its Discontents*, ed. and trans. James Strachey (New York: W. W. Norton, 1961), 78–79.

4. Ibid., 82.

5. Ibid.

6. Sigmund Freud, "Triebe und Triebschicksale" (1915), available in English as "Instincts and Their Vicissitudes," in *The Standard Edition of the Complete Psychological Works of Sigmund Freud*, vol. 14, ed. and trans. James Strachey (London: Hogarth Press, 1957), 109–40.

7. Jean Laplanche, *Life and Death in Psychoanalysis*, trans. Jeffrey Mehlman (Baltimore: Johns Hopkins University Press, 1985).

8. In German: "eine psychologische höchst merkwürdige Überwindung des Triebes, der alles Lebende am Leben festzuhalten zwingt." See Sigmund Freud, "Mourning and Melancholia," in *The Standard Edition*, 14:246; translation mine.

9. Sigmund Freud, "The Economic Problem of Masochism," in *The Standard Edition of the Complete Psychological Works of Sigmund Freud*, vol. 19, ed. and trans. James Strachey (London: Hogarth Press, 1961), 163.

10. Ibid., 164.

11. Ibid.

12. Ibid., 169.

13. Richard Kearney, "Ethics of the Infinite," interview with Emmanuel Levinas (1982), in Richard Cohen, ed., *Face to Face with Levinas* (Albany: State University of New York Press, 1986), 21.

14. Ibid.

15. Ibid., 24.

16. Emmanuel Levinas, *Alterity and Transcendence*, trans. Michael B. Smith (New York: Columbia University Press, 1999), 69.

17. Antonio Negri, "Reliqua Desiderantur: A Conjecture for a Definition of the Concept of Democracy in the Final Spinoza," in Warren Montag and Ted Stolze, eds., *The New Spinoza* (Minneapolis: University of Minnesota Press, 1997).

18. Ibid., 228, 229.

19. Ibid., 230.

20. Ibid., 238.

21. "The mind can neither imagine anything nor recollect past things, except while the body endures. . . . it conceives no body as actually existing except while its body endures." VP21 and P21D, 255.

22. Emmanuel Levinas, *Ethics and Infinity: Conversations with Philippe Nemo*, trans. Richard A. Cohen (Pittsburgh: Duquesne University Press, 1985), 87.

23. Primo Levi, *The Drowned and the Saved*, trans. Raymond Rosenthal (New York: Vintage, 1989), 76.

24. Ibid., 78.

TO SENSE WHAT IS LIVING IN THE OTHER: HEGEL'S EARLY LOVE

1. G. W. F. Hegel, *Early Theological Writings*, trans. T. M. Knox (Chicago: University of Chicago Press, 1948), 302–8. That text was translated from Herman Nohl, *Hegels theologische Jugendschriften* (Tübingen: Mohr, 1907), and a fuller and more annotated text is presently available as a section called "Die Liebe" in "Entwürfe über Religion und Liebe," in *Hegel, Frühe Schriften* (Frankfurt am Main: Suhrkamp, 1986), 239–54.

2. Hegel, *Early Theological Writings*, 309–20; G. W. F. Hegel, "Systemfragment von 1800," in *Frühe Schriften*, 419–27.

3. G. W. F. Hegel, *Hegel's Phenomenology of Spirit*, trans. A. V. Miller (London: Oxford University Press, 1977),58–69; Hegel, *Phänomenologie des Geistes* (Frankfurt am Main: Suhrkamp, 1970), 82–92.

4. Hegel, *Early Theological Writings*, 303–4.

5. Ibid., 303.

6. Hegel, *Early Theological Writings*, 303; *Hegel, Frühe Schriften*, 245.

7. Which religion he is talking about is somewhat vague, but he seems to have in mind the historical development of a certain conjunction of Christianity and Judaism in which the living body of Christ serves as a counterpart to the putatively lifeless laws of Judaism.

8. Hegel, *Early Theological Writings*, 303–4; Hegel, *Frühe Schriften,*245.

9. Hegel, *Frühe Schriften*, 245.

10. Hegel, *Early Theological Writings*, 304; Hegel, *Frühe Schriften*, 245.

11. Hegel, *Early Theological Writings*, 304; Hegel, *Frühe Schriften*, 246.

12. Hegel, Early *Theological Writings*, 305; Hegel, *Frühe Schriften*, 246.

13. Ibid.

14. Hegel, *Early Theological Writings*, 305.

15. Hegel, *Early Theological Writings*, 305; Hegel, *Frühe Schriften*, 246.

16. Hegel's exact language is this: "life senses life . . . since love is a sensing of something living, lovers can be distinct only in so far as they are mortal . . . in lovers there is no matter; they are a living whole." In German: "das Lebendige fühlt das Lebendige. Weil die Liebe ein Gefühl des Lebendigen ist, so

können Liebende sich nur insofern unterscheiden, als sie sterblich sind. . . .
An Liebenden ist keine Materie, sie sind ein lebendiges Ganzes." Hegel, *Early Theological Writings*, 305; Hegel, *Frühe Schriften*, 246.

17. Ibid.
18. Hegel, *Early Theological Writings*, 306; Hegel, *Frühe Schriften*, 247.
19. Ibid.
20. Hegel, *Frühe Schriften*, 247.
21. Hegel, *Early Theological Writings*, 306; Hegel, *Frühe Schriften*, 247.
22. Ibid.
23. Ibid.
24. Ibid.
25. Hegel, *Early Theological Writings*, 308; Hegel, *Frühe Schriften*, 249–50.
26. Hegel, *Early Theological Writings*, 308; Hegel, *Frühe Schriften*, 250.
27. Hegel, *Frühe Schriften*, 421.
28. Hegel, *Early Theological Writings*, 311; Hegel, *Frühe Schriften*, 421.
29. Hegel, *Early Theological Writings*, 316; Hegel, *Frühe Schriften*, 425.
30. Ibid.
31. Hegel, *Early Theological Writings*, 317; Hegel, *Frühe Schriften*, 426.
32. Hegel, *Phenomenology of Spirit*, 27.
33. Ibid. In German: "Das Verschwinden ist vielmehr selbst als wesentlich zu betrachten. . . . Die Erscheinung ist das Entstehen und Verge- hen, das selbst nicht einsteht und vergeht, sondern an sich ist und die Wirklichkeit und Bewegung des Lebens der Wahrheit aus- macht. Das Wahre ist so der bacchantische Taumel, an dem kein Glied nicht trunken ist; und weil jedes, indem es sich absondert, ebenso unmittelbar (sich) aufiöst, ist er ebenso die durchsichtige und einfache Ruhe." Hegel, *Phänomenologie des Geistes*, 46.
34. Quoted in Richard Kroner, "Introduction," in Hegel, *Early Theological Writings*, 38.

KIERKEGAARD'S SPECULATIVE DESPAIR

1. It would be interesting to compare this claim with Freud's efforts to address the question of "anxiety" through analysis.
2. Søren Kierkegaard, *Sickness unto Death*, ed. and trans. Howard V. Hong and Edna H. Hong (Princeton: Princeton University Press, 1983), 14.
3. Ibid., 60.
4. Ibid., 13.

5. "Hegel and Hegelianism constitute an essay in the comical." Søren Kierkegaard, *Concluding Unscientific Postscript*, trans. David F. Swenson and Walter Lowrie (Princeton: Princeton University Press, 1974), 34.

6. "In order to avoid confusion, it is at once necessary to recall that our treatment of the problem does not raise the question of the truth of Christianity. It merely deals with the problem of the individual's relationship to Christianity. It has nothing whatever to do with the systematic zeal of the personally indifferent individual to arrange the truths of Christianity in paragraphs; it deals with the concern of the infinitely interested individual for his own relationship to such a doctrine." Ibid., 18.

7. Descartes, "Meditation V." "God is perfect and can only make what is equally perfect or less perfect than him/her/itself, for nothing can be more perfect than God. If there is something that has some degree of perfection in it, that thing must be produced by what is at least as perfect or more perfect than the thing itself. There is nothing in the world that is more perfect than human beings, even though human beings are imperfect in some ways (they sin, they are ignorant). This implies that human beings must be created by what is equally or more perfect than themselves. And it is that perfect being that is called God."

8. Kierkegaard, *Sickness unto Death*, 13–14.

9. Søren Kierkegaard, *Fear and Trembling / Repetition*, ed. and trans. Howard V. Hong and Edna H. Hong (Princeton: Princeton University Press, 1983), 67.

10. See Kierkegaard's discussion of Abraham in ibid.

11. Søren Kierkegaard, *Philosophical Fragments*, ed. Niels Thulstrop, trans. David F. Swenson and Howard V. Hong (Princeton: Princeton University Press, 1962), 46.

12. Niels Thulstrup, "Commentator's Introduction," in ibid., lxxv.

13. See Kierkegaard's discussion of the limits of speculative thought in *Concluding Unscientific Postscript*, ch. 2, "The Speculative Point of View."

14. Kierkegaard, *Concluding Unscientific Postscript*, 404.

15. Kierkegaard, *Sickness unto Death*, 14.

16. This is a view that is falsely attributed to existential philosophy generally, but that we can see ought not to be ascribed to Kierkegaard.

17. Kierkegaard, *Sickness unto Death*, 15.

18. Kierkegaard, *Fear and Trembling*, 33, 37, 53.

19. Ibid., 36.

20. Ibid.

21. Ibid., 54.

22. Kierkegaard, *Philosophical Fragments*, 99.

23. Kierkegaard, *Fear and Trembling*, 56.

24. It is interesting to note that Kierkegaard takes the phrase "fear and trembling" from the New Testament, Philippians 2:12–14, but applies it to an Old Testament figure, Abraham. Hegel's placement of "fear and trembling" in relation to work is perhaps slightly closer to the meaning of the New Testament use: "Wherefore, my beloved, as ye have always obeyed, not as in my presence only, but now much more in my absence, work out your own salvation with fear and trembling: For it is God which worketh in you both to will and to do of his good pleasure." *The Dartmouth Bible*, ed. Roy B. Chamberlin and Herman Feldman (Boston: Houghton Mifflin, 1961).

25. G. W. F. Hegel, *The Phenomenology of Spirit*, trans. A. V. Miller (New York: Oxford University Press, 1977), 118.

26. Ibid., 119.

27. Imagine if Hegel's bondsman were to have created a son with a woman and that he was then compelled to sacrifice that son, how would Hegel's analysis have to change in order to take account of Abraham's anguish?

28. Kierkegaard, *Fear and Trembling*, 41.

29. Note Kierkegaard's ironic tone in his writing against the historical efforts to supply a proof of God's existence: "And how does the God's existence emerge from the proof? Does it follow straightway, without any breach of continuity? . . . As long as I keep my hold on the proof, i.e. continue to demonstrate, the existence does not come out, if for no other reason than that I am engaged in proving it; but when I let the proof go, the existence is there. But this act of letting go is surely also something; it is indeed a contribution of mine. Must not this also be taken into account, this little moment, brief as it may be—it need not be long, for it is a leap. However brief this moment, if only an instantaneous now, this 'now' must be included in the reckoning." Kierkegaard, *Philosophical Fragments*, 53.

Kierkegaard here plays on the double meaning of the act of letting go being "a contribution of mine." On the one hand, this is his philosophical contribution to the critique of rationalism, and "the leap" is a concept he introduced into philosophical and religious discourse. On the other hand, he is suggesting that no person, including himself, can arrive at faith without making a contribution of himself or herself. And this contribution, being one of passion, has to come from the inwardness of the self, and be directed toward a faith that no "proof" can automatically produce.

30. Ibid., 21–23.

31. See Louis Mackey, *Kierkegaard: A Kind of Poet* (Philadelphia: University of Pennsylvania Press, 1971).

32. Kierkegaard, *Sickness unto Death*, 68.

33. Ibid.

34. Ibid., 69.

35. Ibid.

36. Ibid., 74.

37. Quoted in the introduction to *Concluding Unscientific Postscript*, xiii.

SEXUAL DIFFERENCE AS A QUESTION OF ETHICS:
ALTERITIES OF THE FLESH IN IRIGARAY AND
MERLEAU-PONTY

This essay was originally written in 1990. The publication of the translation of Luce Irigaray's *An Ethics of Sexual Difference* (trans. Carolyn Burke and Gillian C. Gill [Ithaca: Cornell University Press, 1993]) offered the opportunity for English-speaking readers to consider her most sustained considerations of the history of philosophy. The text is composed of a set of lectures, ranging from chapters on Plato's *Symposium* and Aristotle's *Physics* to Descartes's *The Passions of the Soul*, Spinoza on God, and a final set of reflections on Merleau-Ponty's posthumously published *The Visible and the Invisible* and Emmanuel Levinas's *Totality and Infinity*.

1. Martin Heidegger, *Being and Time*, trans. John Macquarrie and Edward Robinson (New York: Harper and Row, 1962), 24–25.

2. Maurice Merleau-Ponty, *The Visible and the Invisible*, trans. Alphonso Lingis (Evanston: Northwestern University Press, 1968), 146.

3. Irigaray, *An Ethics of Sexual Difference*, 157.

4. Ibid., 173.

5. Ibid., 161–62.

6. Merleau-Ponty, *The Visible and the Invisible*, 155.

7. Ibid., 154.

8. Irigaray, *An Ethics of Sexual Difference*, 178.

9. Ibid.

10. Ibid., 183.

11. Merleau-Ponty, *The Visible and the Invisible*, 147–48.

VIOLENCE, NONVIOLENCE: SARTRE ON FANON

This paper was presented at the 2005 Hannah Arendt / Reiner Schür-
mann Symposium for Political Philosophy at The New School for Social
Research. The author wishes to express enormous gratitude for the editorial
assistance of Colleen Pearl and Amy Huber.

1. Jean-Paul Sartre, "Preface," in Frantz Fanon, *The Wretched of the Earth*,
trans. Constance Farrington (New York: Grove Press, 1963). At the wish of
Fanon's widow, Sartre's preface was withdrawn from the 1967 edition, though
it does seem to appear in subsequent editions. Unless explicitly noted,
citations are to the 1963 edition.

2. For a further elaboration of this position, see my *Giving an Account of
Oneself* (New York: Fordham University Press, 2005).

3. See Orlando Patterson, *Slavery and Social Death: A Comparative Study*
(Cambridge, MA: Harvard University Press, 1982); and Abdul JanMohamed,
The Death-Bound Subject (Durham: Duke University Press, 2005).

4. Homi Bhabha, "Framing Fanon," foreword to Frantz Fanon, *The
Wretched of the Earth*, trans. Richard Philcox (New York: Grove Press, 2004), xi.

5. See Walter Benjamin on the divine violence that obliterates the traces of
guilt in "The Meaning of Time in the Moral Universe," in *Walter Benjamin:
Selected Writings Volume 1, 1913–26*, ed. Marcus Bullock and Michael W. Jennings
(Cambridge, MA: Harvard University Press, 1996), 286–87.

6. Sartre does not name Camus explicitly, but he is clearly referring to,
among others, "Le socialisme des potences" and "Le pari de notre genera-
tion" that appeared in *Demain* in 1957 and that have been translated by Justin
O'Brien and republished in *Albert Camus: Resistance, Rebellion, and Death* (New
York: Random House, 1995).

7. Ronald Santoni, *Sartre on Violence: Curiously Ambivalent* (University Park:
Pennsylvania State University Press, 2003),67–74.

8. See Rey Chow, *Primitive Passions* (New York: Columbia University Press,
1995).

9. Frantz Fanon, *Black Skin, White Masks*, trans. Charles Lam Markmann
(New York: Grove Press, 1967), 232.

10. Michel Contat and Jean-Paul Sartre, "Sartre at Seventy: An Interview,"
trans. Paul Auster and Lydia Davis, *New York Review of Books* 22, no. 13
(August 7, 1975).

11. Jean-Paul Sartre, *Life/Situations: Essays Written and Spoken*, trans. Paul
Auster and Lydia Davis (New York: Pantheon Books, 1977), 11–12.

12. Hannah Arendt, *The Human Condition* (Chicago: University of Chicago Press, 1958), 183.

13. Adriana Caverero, *Relating Narratives: Story-Telling and Selfhood*, trans. Paul Kottman (London: Routledge, 2000), 90–91: "The 'you' comes before the *we*, before the plural *you* and before the *they*. Symptomatically, the 'you' is a term that is not at home in modern and contemporary developments of ethics and politics. The 'you' is ignored by individualistic doctrines, which are too preoccupied with praising the rights of the *I*, and the 'you' is masked by a Kantian form of ethics that is only capable of staging an *I* that addresses itself as a familiar 'you'. Neither does the 'you' find a home in the schools of thought to which individualism is opposed—these schools reveal themselves for the most part to be affected by a moralistic vice, which, in order to avoid falling into the decadence of the *I*, avoids the contiguity of the *you*, and privileges collective, plural pronouns. Indeed, many revolutionary movements (which range from traditional communism to the feminism of sisterhood) seem to share a curious linguistic code based on the intrinsic morality of pronouns. The *we* is always positive, the plural *you* is a possible ally, the *they* has the face of an antagonist, the *I* is unseemly, and the *you* is, of course, superfluous."

INDEX